TWENTY MINUTES WITH THE DEVIL

LUIS GÓMEZ ROMERO & DESMOND MANDERSON

CURRENCY PRESS
The performing arts publisher

CURRENT THEATRE SERIES

First published in 2021
by Currency Press Pty Ltd,
PO Box 2287, Strawberry Hills, NSW, 2012, Australia
enquiries@currency.com.au
www.currency.com.au

in association with The Street, Canberra

Typeset by Dean Nottle for Currency Press.
Cover features PJ Williams, photo by Creswick Collective, design by DAMS.

Currency Press acknowledges the Traditional Owners of the Country on which
we live and work. We pay our respects to all Aboriginal and Torres Strait
Islander Elders, past and present.

A catalogue record for this
book is available from the
National Library of Australia

Contents

I like to walk in the mountains	*Me gusta andar por la sierra*
I grew up in the bush	*me crié entre los matorrales*
where I learnt maths	*allí aprendí a hacer las cuentas*
just by counting sacks.	*nomás contando costales.*
I like to get away from the nets	*Me gusta burlar las redes*
cast by the feds	*que tienden los federales*

—Teodoro Bello
Pacas de a kilo (narcocorrido)

They are monsters,	*¡Son monstruos,*
I'm surrounded by monsters!	*estoy cercado de monstruos!*
They do not devour me.	*No me devoran.*
They devour my yearned repose,	*Devoran mi reposo anhelado,*
they shape me into a self-developing anguish,	*me hacen ser una angustia que se desarrolla a sí misma,*
they make me a man,	*me hacen hombre,*
a monster among monsters.	*monstruo entre monstruos.*

—Dámaso Alonso
Hijos de la Ira

Twenty Minutes with the Devil was first produced by at The Street Theatre, Canberra, on 21 August 2021, with the following cast:

EL TICHO	PJ Williams
ANGELA BASSOLS GUZMÁN	Joanna Richards
RÓMULO GARCÍA HERNÁNDEZ	Raoul Craemer

Director, Caroline Stacey
Production Design, Imogen Keen
Sound Design, James Tighe
Lighting Design, Antony Hateley
Movement, Zsuzsi Soboslay
Stage Manager, Brittany Myers

CHARACTERS

PATRICIO JESÚS HORTENSIO PRIETO CHÁVEZ, aka EL TICHO or JESÚS: Southern businessman and drug lord. About 60, short, dark-skinned, stocky, dressed in a long singlet that is covered in shit, long johns and sneakers.

ANGELA BASSOLS GUZMÁN: Police officer. Mid-30s, pale-skinned, blonde. She is dressed in an impeccable blue military-style uniform with brilliant leather patrol boots and a bulky police vest. The word 'POLICÍA' is printed across its back. She wears a cross on a thin golden chain around her neck, which she touches nervously from time to time. She is armed with a semi-automatic pistol.

RÓMULO GARCÍA HERNÁNDEZ: Police officer. Maybe a little older than Angela, dark-skinned, medium height, asthmatic. His uniform and boots are by no means immaculate. He is wearing a jacket with multiple pockets; the word 'POLICÍA' is printed above the front pocket. He is armed with a semi-automatic rifle which he carries in a sling. He has a tattoo of a green bird with a red breast on his arm.

SETTING

Cheap hotel room, tackily decorated. Double bed, small white blanket on the end. Small bedside table and clock radio, flashing 12:00 a.m. Kitchenette and coffee machine with two cups stage left, bar fridge, rubbish bin, old air conditioning unit. Window, upstage centre, covered by a heavy curtain. Downstage, a coffee table with some cheap magazines and a mobile phone on it, two chairs. Main entrance upstage left with a fading sign on the door: 'PROHIBIDO FUMAR'. A small door leading to an offstage bathroom downstage right.

A NOTE ON THE TEXT

Lines that should run on without a pause are indicated by the symbol —

Lines that should overlap are indicated by the symbol /

SCENE ONE: THE HOSPITALITY BUSINESS

Rhythmic flapping sounds, like a distant helicopter—or a moth. A single candle or bright light; moth wings cast anamorphic shadows on the walls.

Spotlight—a man, hands tied with metal handcuff, leg cuffed to a bed. A big black moth has landed on his hand and he examines it. EL TICHO *appears to be talking to it.*

EL TICHO: Where I'm from, nothing's on your side. The sun is too strong. The soil is too hard. The wind twists the trees and makes them cry. For all the fuckin' good crying does. No roads, no doctors, no teachers, not even a mouldy priest. That's where it starts. Where it ends up, who can say? A beach; a city; north, south; it gets around more than I do. I'm just a glorified travel agent. You think that's easy? Someone's out to screw you, every step of the way. The competition, the government. My boys, I pay them good money but even they are not always to be trusted.

> *He raises his hand to look closely at the moth, then tries to blow or shake it off. The moth does not budge.*

You see, my friend, I am a humble businessman with a knack for success and no time for weakness. Things don't always go according to plan. Don't flap around, feeling sorry for yourself. You want to survive, you need to adapt. Sometimes there is collateral damage. Just be sure, at the end of the day, the collateral damage is not you. It's a risky business, but then again, all business is risky.

> *He suddenly slaps the moth with his right hand. The moth falls, dead. Blackout.*

> *The wing shadows, accompanied by the flapping sound, move closer to the candlelight. The sound of crackling fire.*

> *Lights up.* EL TICHO *is sitting between* RÓMULO *and* ANGELA.

RÓMULO: [*wearing earbuds*] *¿Qué hacemos aquí?*

ANGELA: [*nervously touching the cross around her neck*] *Nuestro trabajo.*

EL TICHO: *Quiero presentar una queja formal.*

There is a slight shift in the light, like the sun coming from behind a cloud. We are entering another world—a world in translation.

RÓMULO: What are we doing here?

ANGELA: Our job.

EL TICHO: I wish to file a formal complaint.

> RÓMULO *takes a pack of cigarettes out of his pocket.*

ANGELA: You know the law forbids smoking in a hospitality facility, Sergeant.

RÓMULO: We're in the hospitality business now?

> RÓMULO *takes out a bag of crisps and a sachet of chilli sauce which he squeezes on them. He puts the earbuds in and starts listening to loud salsa music*

Hoo, that's some hot sauce I reckon. Waddya say, Boss. Want some?

ANGELA: I'm fine.

RÓMULO: I said, this *salsa Adelita*, man—

ANGELA: I *said*— [*pulling his earbuds off*] —I'll save my taste buds— if it's all the same to you.

> ANGELA *starts to gingerly inspect the room and straighten things up. She looks at the clock radio, checks the time by her own watch, and corrects it. She places the clock back on the bedside table. The characters should be able to see the digits, but the audience should not.*

RÓMULO: Waddya saving 'em for? A rainy day?

ANGELA: It's poison.

RÓMULO: One man's poison is another man's meat, know what I'm sayin'?

ANGELA: [*under her breath*] *Cholo* food.

RÓMULO: Are you for fucking real, lady? Hot chilli sauce, it runs in our veins. Where you *from*?

ANGELA: As if you didn't know.

RÓMULO: Oh wait, right, cold as a nun's pussy up in the highlands, man. Mother Mary.

> ANGELA *bristles.*

I couldn't stand it. Ice is for drinks.

ANGELA: All you get in this place is sleet and acid rain. My father was posted to the North one year, though, when I was a girl. Snow on the mountains, like a fresh white blanket over everything. I'd never seen anything so beautiful.

[*Interior voice*] *Making angels in the snow, papa. Blood-splashed angels.*

RÓMULO: Yeah, well, the old man was no big shot so I guess I missed out on the ski trips.

ANGELA: True, Sergeant, we come from different worlds, you and I. *No sea igualado.*

RÓMULO: Come again? You know, I'm not the one who's into the law, Boss, but I'm pretty sure you can't go round saying shit like that.

ANGELA: Stating the obvious is not a crime, Sergeant García.

RÓMULO: Different worlds? Shit, you got that right. I like my sun like my chilli—so hot you can feel it burn.

ANGELA: Is this one of those real man things—?

RÓMULO: Tell ya what, I'll stop acting like a real man if you stop actin' like a real—a—a real—

ANGELA: Like a real commanding officer, Sergeant?

She takes out a notebook.

EL TICHO: Well, as the superior officer, *señora*—

RÓMULO: What are you doin', man?

ANGELA: I'm taking notes.

RÓMULO: Notes about what?

ANGELA: Notes about you.

RÓMULO: What? About me? About what about me?

ANGELA: About your attitude. Not to mention your language.

RÓMULO: Jesus … fucking … oh, man…

ANGELA: I have been advised to keep a paper trail.

RÓMULO: What the fuckin'—what for?

ANGELA: Let us just say, to fully document your ability. To monitor your performance.

RÓMULO: What is this? Boot camp? The army?

ANGELA: If only. They know the importance of discipline in the army. We could learn a thing or two from them, that's for sure.

RÓMULO: Hey, I got nothin' to prove, a man of my calibre.

He pats his rifle in a lame gesture.

Chilli. It's not about the pain. It's like that song, you know? Life gives you surprises, and surprises give you life.

ANGELA: If you say so.

RÓMULO: [*sucking the sauce off a crisp right in her face*] It's one of life's hot salty surprises. You should try it, man.

ANGELA: You like surprises? Look around.

EL TICHO: [*asking what appears to be a question, in a tone he will often employ, to make a demand*] For how long do you plan on keeping me here?

ANGELA: Until we're told. *Señor*. Shouldn't be much longer.

RÓMULO: Headquarters…

He gets up and tries to get the air conditioning to work, with rising frustration.

I'm not holding my breath. Though you smell so ripe, man, what choice we got?

EL TICHO: Is this a joke to you—?

RÓMULO: Could be. Depends on the punch line.

EL TICHO: I am serious. I have never been so humiliated in my life. I need clean clothes.

ANGELA: I'm afraid not, sir. Evidence.

EL TICHO: *Evidence?* Evidence of what?

RÓMULO: Sewage spill? Dirty weekend? Sure, that must be it. Bet that perfume of yours drives the *chicas* wild, man. Am I right? *Eau de toilette*—

EL TICHO: Or at the very least, a shower—

RÓMULO: Get it? Get it?—Toilet water, see?

ANGELA: Sergeant, *basta*—

RÓMULO: Hey, you writing this down, Boss? Don't want my jokes goin' to waste.

ANGELA: Grab a wet towel from the bathroom and give him a sponge bath.

RÓMULO: You gotta be kiddin' me.

ANGELA: You heard me. Let's get this over with before we all choke to death on the methane. He smells to high heaven.

RÓMULO: No fuckin' problem, Boss. Cleaning up other people's shit, that's what we *cholos* are good for, right?

ANGELA: Don't be ridiculous.

RÓMULO *exits to bathroom offstage, leaving his rifle leaning against the door. Sound of a tap running.*

RÓMULO: [*offstage*] Know what, I have no problems with the smell of shit. I grew up with it.

ANGELA: I'm well aware.

RÓMULO *returns with a wet towel.*

RÓMULO: I wasn't talking to you, Lieutenant. You don't know what shit is.

ANGELA: [*writing in her notebook*] Well, I'm sure you two have a great deal in common. Just clean him up as best you can and make it snappy.

RÓMULO *begins to wipe him down. During the following conversation,* EL TICHO *stares into the middle distance, but gradually pays attention to what* RÓMULO *is doing.*

RÓMULO: Grew up right next to the biggest dump in the whole city, man. Wind blew in the wrong direction, you could smell it. Fuck, wind blew any old direction you'd smell it, man.

EL TICHO: Is that a fact.

RÓMULO: [*rolling up one of his sleeves, revealing a tattoo*] That's what this is for. So I don't forget where I'm from, man.

EL TICHO: Some kind of bird, is it?

RÓMULO: A story. An old story. Make believe. I guess… [*Interior voice*] *Sponging him like the old man. Viejo pendejo.*

For a moment, there is a relaxation in EL TICHO*'s body, a study of his muscles in* RÓMULO*'s actions. Power hovers between* RÓMULO*'s servitude and* EL TICHO*'s vulnerability. Suddenly, the spell is broken.* ROMULO *steps away.*

EL TICHO: You missed a bit, son.

RÓMULO: Lick it off yourself, *señor.*

He throws the towel on the bed.

ANGELA: Are you going to leave that lying around, Sergeant?

RÓMULO: You gonna take notes 'bout my personal hygiene too?

ANGELA: No, I think we better focus on areas where we can hope for improvement.

RÓMULO: Think I was born dirty, Boss?

ANGELA: Not at all, I just think you've had plenty of practice.

RÓMULO: Reckon I better get a notebook of my own, Lieutenant.

He snatches the towel up, exits to the bathroom. Sound of a tap running.

EL TICHO: What is this place?

ANGELA: It's a motel.

EL TICHO: I can see that.

ANGELA: I believe it's called 'The Soft Touch'.

EL TICHO: Is it? I can't wait to hear what the Human Rights Commissioner has to say about your touch, Officer, which is far from soft—

ANGELA: The incident / has been reported—

EL TICHO: What 'incident'? My colleague Víctor and I are driving down the highway. Late, not another car in sight—

ANGELA: We clocked you doing 130 / in a hundred zone, *señor*.

EL TICHO: Do you expect me to believe that this is someone's mad idea of a speeding blitz, *señora*?

ANGELA: I'll ask the questions here, *señor*—

EL TICHO: By what authority do you photograph me without my consent, without my consent I assure you?

ANGELA: If you don't have any identification papers, it's hardly surprising that we sent through a photo. If you're in the database, *señor*, we'll find out who you are soon enough. So why don't you save everyone some time—?

EL TICHO: You leave my driver out there—handcuffed to the steering wheel like a tethered goat. You know it's not safe in the desert when the stars and the cockroaches come out. Tell me, *señora*, is he your prisoner or is he bait?

ANGELA moves a chair beside the bed and begins an interrogation.

ANGELA: Okay, *señor*, you need to calm down. Let's start with / your name—

EL TICHO: You haul me off the street. You take me to some sleazy motel room. You tie me up half-naked—

RÓMULO: [*re-entering*] Par for the course in this joint, / don't ya reckon?—

EL TICHO: Since when has the Highway Patrol stopped arresting people and started kidnapping them?

ANGELA: Hey! Name!

EL TICHO: [*snapping*] I am El Ticho.

> *Sudden silence. Then* ANGELA *and* RÓMULO *burst into gales of laughter.*

RÓMULO: The most wanted man in the country, my bum crack. It's way past knock-off time, I shoulda been off duty already, I'm meant to pick up my little girl. So cut the crap, man, we all know this has fuck-all to do with your driving. Look at you. Some weird shit has gone down tonight, man, that's for fucking sure, and it's just my lousy luck that we're the ones stuck with mopping it up. Tell me, Mister Mystery, who are you—?

ANGELA: Just answer the question, sir—

EL TICHO: Have it your way. My name is Jesús. / I am sixty years old.

RÓMULO: *Jesús.* Hear that, Lieutenant? Praise the Lord, we're saved—!

ANGELA: Let's not bring the Lord into this, / Sergeant—

RÓMULO: He started it, man.

EL TICHO: I am a farmer. A farmer and a businessman—

ANGELA: And the guns in your car—?

EL TICHO: I hunt from time to time.

RÓMULO: Oh, that's *camouflage* you're wearing.

> RÓMULO *picks up the phone from the coffee table and proceeds to examine it carefully.*

EL TICHO: Feral pigs, mostly.

ANGELA: No, *señor*, you'll have to do better than that. We find you hiding under a rug on the back seat, dressed in nothing but a soiled singlet—

RÓMULO: And the briefcase—?

ANGELA: What briefcase—?

RÓMULO: *No importa.*

ANGELA: What are you *doing*? Haven't you heard of the chain of evidence? Oh wait, you *skipped* that workshop.

RÓMULO: Waste of time, man. What I'm tryin' to figure is how come our farmer here got a fancy new phone but only one contact. You got no friends, man? See, bad B.O. will do that.

EL TICHO: Since I do not appear to be under arrest, I would like my phone back.

ANGELA: No-one touches the phone. We follow procedure, is that clear? Sergeant, here …

She takes a Ziploc bag from a pocket.

Forensics might need it later.

RÓMULO *places the mobile phone in the Ziploc bag, and puts it back on the table.*

RÓMULO: One call. Half an hour ago, give or take. To 'Father'.

EL TICHO: I wish to let him know I will be late for dinner—

RÓMULO: Tell ya what, El Stinko—figure you're gonna be late for dinner? You're gonna be late for *breakfast*—

EL TICHO: You know people like you have lost their badges for less.

RÓMULO: [*drawing* ANGELA *to one side*] He's right, man. Last thing we want is those turds from the Human Rights Commission shovin' their noses up our arses like a pack of randy dogs.

ANGELA: Since when do you care?

RÓMULO: Since I don't want this smelly *pendejo* to cost me my job. Holy fuckin' Mary, I just want outta here. Boss, I've got a bad feeling.

ANGELA: We're not paid to have feelings. We're paid to do our job.

RÓMULO: I saw something. On the lamp downstairs. [*Sotto voce*] *La bruja negra*—the black witch—

ANGELA: Sergeant!—Are you *high* on that chilli of yours?

RÓMULO: *La mariposa de la muerte*—

ANGELA: Sergeant, you're talking about a moth? You saw a moth?

RÓMULO: It's *La Santa Muerte*.

ANGELA: Great. Bag it up and we'll send it off to forensics / with the rest.

RÓMULO: You don't mess with *La Santa Muerte*, man.

ANGELA: ¡*Por Dios*!

She takes out a notebook.

RÓMULO: You putting this in your damn memoirs, man?

ANGELA: I have better things to do with my time than listen to your foolish old wives' tales, Sergeant.

RÓMULO: Yeah, well you can write this down and all, man. Someone's gonna die here tonight. I can feel it in my bones. The black witch is coming for one of us—

His phone rings.

And here she is, right on fucking cue.

He exits to the bathroom and talks through the closed door.

Hello? Yeah, look, I'm sorry, I got a little held up … Half an hour, tops … Listen, baby, think I don't know what day of the week it is? … Oh, *¡que te jodan—!*

He re-enters.

Fucking *bitch.*

He hurls his phone across the room, and immediately picks it up again.

Now she broke my phone.

ANGELA: Who was that?

RÓMULO: Who do *you* think?

ANGELA: Something about your daughter …

RÓMULO: Her *mother.* Says it's a school night—

EL TICHO: Ah. Mothers.

RÓMULO: She'll go back to court. She'll say I can't be trusted. She'll stop me seeing my own kid. Fuck that bitch! It's not fucking fair. What about my rights? What about me?

ANGELA: A police officer and a family, no-one said it was easy.

RÓMULO: You don't miss a trick, eh Lieutenant?

ANGELA: I'm your supervisor.

RÓMULO: Man, bet you fuckin' aced the workshop / on that.

EL TICHO: Listen, Captain—

ANGELA: Lieutenant—

EL TICHO: What you say is correct. My colleague should not have broken the law. Believe me, my dear, I will take it up with him personally. Write me out a ticket, take down my details in that excellent book of yours, and we can all go home …

RÓMULO: You know, Boss, if I left now—

EL TICHO: None of this will hold up in court, *señora.* I think you know that—

ANGELA: [*edging unwittingly close to* EL TICHO] Well, I … I … No, no—

EL TICHO: [*making a sudden grab for her arm*] Don't you know who I am—?

ANGELA: [*pulling away in disgust*] How *dare* you—!

RÓMULO: Oh, piss on a fucking tree why don't you? Every douchebag in the fuckin' land says the same thing. *Don't you know who I am*—

{
  EL TICHO: No, I mean it.—

  ANGELA: Not this again—

  RÓMULO: Like that coke-head *mirrey*. Son of a bitch out cruisin' in his SUV. Fucker ploughed / right into that cyclist, man—in a *bike* lane for Chrissake. / Guy's lyin' in the road—All smashed up, / rolling round in the gutter—and Don Bicycle cocksucker in his SUV makes like it's all a big fuckin' joke. *Hey, dude, don't you know who I am*—?

ANGELA: I was there too, if you recall.

RÓMULO: Were you? Were you? 'Dude'. Prick treats me like a lump of dog turd stuck to the bottom of his shiny new shoes. Sails off like I'm not even there. What were you even doing, fiddling with your phone the whole time—?

ANGELA: Texting his licence plate / to the station—

RÓMULO: Updating your Facebook status? / Swiping right?

ANGELA: Hey! Sergeant! I've had quite enough out of you. This is what I'm talking about. I write it down and you go on report. *¿Entendido?*

RÓMULO: License plate. Get real, Boss—

ANGELA: Truth is, we'd have traced him by now. If you'd bothered to do the paperwork.

RÓMULO: You and I both know how this plays out. The suits turn up like vultures at a butcher's shop. Phone calls are made. Hands are shaken. Game fucking over.

ANGELA: Just fill in the forms, for crying out loud.

RÓMULO: Fucking bullshit. Only thing these needle-dicks understand is a well-aimed kick in the *huevos*, teach 'em they can't diss *el tira*, man.

    He picks up his rifle.

Chilli? Hotter the fuckin' better. Reckon the pain in the mouth makes me forget the pains in the butt.

EL TICHO: Pardon me but your dramas are not my concern. *Tengo derechos, señor.*

RÓMULO: [*grabbing him roughly*] You shitty half-pint—You want rights? You want the Constitution? [*Tapping the rifle*] This is your

Constitution—and tell ya what, I'm gonna breech-load those fuckin'
rights / right up—

ANGELA: *¡Ya basta!* Sergeant! Step away from the suspect now!

RÓMULO: Where's the fun in that?

ANGELA: Fun is not my job. Law's my job.

RÓMULO: No shit.

> *During the following,* RÓMULO *struggles to open the window
> wider. He takes a* paliacate *from his pocket, wipes his brow and
> drapes it over the back of a chair. Then comes and stands over*
> EL TICHO.

Ah, what's the use, Boss? We both know this dung beetle is up to no
good. He's gonna say *nada* till his lawyer shows up, just like the rest
of 'em. And a smelly little man like you, Don Long John, reckon you
gonna need two lawyers for sure!

> ANGELA's *phone rings. She moves to one side to take the call.
> She is focused so intently that she pays no attention to* RÓMULO
> *until the call ends.* RÓMULO *for his part is paying attention only
> to* EL TICHO.

EL TICHO: I rarely lose my temper
but for you, my friend, I may
make an exception.

> ANGELA: Lieutenant Bassols.
> Yes—

> ANGELA *moves to check the room number.*

RÓMULO: You're a bit of a fatberg,
anyone ever told you that?

> RÓMULO *slaps* EL TICHO *across the face.* EL TICHO *freezes.*

> ANGELA: We're in one-o-one …
> You've got his ID? Already?

EL TICHO: Strike one.

> ANGELA: Wait … *Who?*

> RÓMULO *gives* EL TICHO *a much harder slap*

> ANGELA: Oh Lord, you've got to
> be joking. Are you sure? Are
> you absolutely positive?

EL TICHO: Strike two.

RÓMULO *grabs* EL TICHO's *hair. Pulls his head back sharply and moves in close.*

RÓMULO: What is it you're not telling us, sweet pea?

RÓMULO: You wanna suck my nightstick with that chubby dickface of yours?

ANGELA: Oh, sweet Jesus Christ. So what now?

ANGELA: *Entendido ... Claro ...*

ANGELA: The army? *How long ...?* Oh, dear Lord. Let me speak to the captain, okay?

ANGELA: Captain? I need backup *right now* ... There's only the two of us, and that's including Sergeant García ... I see ... [*Stealing a glance at the clock*] Yessir. Yessir. Just gone eleven-forty. So—

The clock is deceitful though. Time dilation occurs—an emotional analogue to Einstein's special theory of relativity. Time appears to move more slowly for those drawn into the gravitational field of the crisis—our characters—than to outside observers.

RÓMULO: [*very close to* EL TICHO *now*] Waddya say, *señor?*

RÓMULO: Reckon my *macana* will loosen your *lengua?* Mmm ...

ANGELA: *Claro, Capitán.*

ANGELA *hangs up; silence.*

It is the sudden silence that RÓMULO *notices. He turns to* ANGELA.

ANGELA: *Dios mío, Dios mío.*

EL TICHO: My name is Patricio
Jesús Hortensio Prieto
Chávez. I am called El Ticho.

Blackout.

SCENE TWO: OUTGUNNED

A spotlight on EL TICHO.

EL TICHO: Tunnels are my business. Saves time at the border, I find. The one that got me out of our so-called maximum-security prison— piped music, air conditioning, a big black Harley for the getaway. Just like the movies. No, better. Where I am from, they've never heard of Hollywood, but they've fucking heard of me.

Actors. You think you can trust somebody who pretends to be somebody else? Arranging to meet up with that TV star was a big mistake, *carajo.* Well, she turned me on, what can I say. Fuckin' Northern show pony who tagged along for the ride, not so much. Cocksucker can't even take a piss without admiring his dick, led half the fucking army right to my fucking door. Sons of bitches thought they were in the movies too, playing cowboys and Indians for real. Fuck them and fuck their mothers.

You don't think I had a plan? There's always a plan. Under the bath and down into the sewers. Tunnels, you see, we're back to tunnels. Do you fear the dark? Good. That is what darkness is for. It's pitch black in front, pitch black behind. You don't know where you are. Perhaps you fear a nasty surprise down there, my friend. Not me. I'm at home in the wet black guts of this world. I finally popped out into the night air again like a turd out of some huge concrete arsehole. So what, so fuckin' what. I fucking showed them what useless arse-licking faggots they are. They should let me run the country. Correction. They already do.

It all goes off without a hitch until—until. Till the fucking road-runners turn up, about as welcome as a couple of maggots on a steak. And for what? For what? It's *this* fucking country. It's the middle of the night. Who doesn't break the fucking speed limit? Fucking unbelievable.

The human factor will always let you down. Believe me. In my game there is no room for error. The product must be at the right place at the right time. If you can't be relied on then I have no use for you. I will cut my losses.

He mimes shooting someone.

Call it on-the-job training.

I will let you in on a secret. After a while, you don't need a gun. The idea of a gun works better, I find. No wasted bullets. Reputation has always been central in my line of work. Maybe that makes me an actor too. But smarter. *¿Tú me entiendes, verdad?*

Lights up. Sound of retching from the bathroom. ANGELA *is checking the room with anxious precision, straightening the magazines.* RÓMULO *comes out of the bathroom without his rifle.* ANGELA *exits to the bathroom.* RÓMULO *slumps down, putting his feet up on the table.*

ANGELA: [*offstage*] For heaven's sake, you could have flushed.

She re-enters.

Close that window.

RÓMULO: Oh man, no. It's like having sex on a plastic sheet in here. In a public toilet.

ANGELA: I wouldn't know.

RÓMULO: I got asthma or something, man, I don't breathe so good.

ANGELA: Shut the windows, close the curtains, secure the perimeter—
You know the drill. Let's do it right.

RÓMULO *sullenly closes the window, with some difficulty.*

That's that. The army's on its way—

RÓMULO: How long, man?

ANGELA: Twenty minutes they said; twelve o'clock—

RÓMULO: [*glancing at the clock, then at* EL TICHO] He warned me, I should have known. I saw the signs; the wind was blowing like the Lash of St. Francis out there. It's a bad omen, man … Fuck, what a mess.

ANGELA: Feeling better?

RÓMULO: For Chrissakes, I'm not talking about the chilli. We're stuck here, man, in between the wildcat and the coyotes.

They sit at the coffee table. El Ticho's phone rings.

EL TICHO: That's my phone.

RÓMULO: I'll get it—

ANGELA: *Stop*. Do not touch that phone. That's an order, Sergeant.

RÓMULO: C'mon, man. Answer the goddamn phone. Hostage negotiation workshop—what was that about?

ANGELA: It wasn't about taking hostages, it was about releasing them.

RÓMULO: So you're so smart, release us why don't you.

> *The phone stops.* EL TICHO *quickly glances at the clock.*

ANGELA: They gave us strict instructions—don't talk to him, don't call anyone, don't answer the phone, just wait. We have our orders, Sergeant.

RÓMULO: Oh man, this is not good.

ANGELA: They don't trust the narcos.

RÓMULO: Get real, *jefa*, they don't trust *us*. You think they're acting in our best interests? Please. They've got their own best interests. We're just—what's it called?

EL TICHO: Collateral damage.

> *The phone rings again. They stare at it until it stops.*

I don't suppose it was for you. I suppose it was for me.

RÓMULO: Oh God—I need a drink, man, take notes if you want, I don't care—

> *He goes to the bar fridge, eventually wrenches it open. It is empty. He slams it shut.*

What kind of a one-star fleabag is this place anyway? Why couldn't we have picked him up outside a Hilton for fuck's sake?

ANGELA: Come here, Officer. [*Speaking in a low voice*] *Pull yourself together*. I don't want to have to tell you again.

RÓMULO: Don't you see, Chief? Stop and think. Figure we're the only ones who've called for backup? He made a call. He called Father.

ANGELA: Father.

RÓMULO: Father, nothin'—the whole tribe's on its way, brothers and sisters and kissing cousins. What we saw out there—that was small beer. These motherfuckers are armed to the teeth and then some, man. You reckon this time they're gonna pull over for the fuckin' *highway* patrol, man? Which, by the way, is not even out patrolling the highway no more, it's baled up here in the only bone-dry love hotel in all the world, and we got nothin' to bring to the firefight, 'cept a couple of lousy popguns and not enough ammo. Oh, and a crucifix, how could I forget?

ANGELA: [*taking out her notebook*] Keep your blasphemies to yourself, Sergeant.

RÓMULO: Jesus, man, you filing a copy with God?

ANGELA: Where's your weapon, anyway?

RÓMULO: *¡Mierda!*

He goes to get it. The phone rings as he returns.

Shut up, shut *up*—

EL TICHO: Pick up the phone, you pussies—

RÓMULO *is waving the rifle wildly.*

ANGELA: Stop waving that thing around, will you?

The phone stops.

We just have to wait till the army turns up. [*Glancing at the clock*] I've told you, they'll be here by midnight.

RÓMULO: Fuck me dead, you got GPS in that *medallita* round your neck? Where d'ya get that idea from?

ANGELA: HQ told me.

RÓMULO: Yeah, and who told them? His guys, our guys. Watch TV and it's like they're on opposite sides, but you and I both know it's not that simple. One day they're trying to wipe each other out, the next they're wiping each other's arses.

ANGELA: It is simple, Sergeant. We do as we're told.

RÓMULO: Oh, c'mon! Drugs. Shit. Man, the whole station's fucking riddled with it. Using it and selling it / and trading it—

ANGELA: He's not some two-bit hustler!

EL TICHO: Thank you, sweetheart.

RÓMULO: I *know*. I'm not talking about those clowns down in the evidence room, taking their slice likes it's part of the fuckin' pension plan. I'm not talking about some *sicario* or *mula* getting what's coming to them—

ANGELA: We're talking about the *army*—

RÓMULO: Yeah, right. A whole busload of students vanishes into thin air, never seen again, man—all happens right under the nose of the military. Chrissakes, you don't reckon the army and the *narcos* were sucking each other off over that one?

ANGELA: That's absurd—

RÓMULO: Only 'coz it's fuckin' true!

ANGELA: I know those people. They know what they're doing.

RÓMULO: Sure thing, Boss, bet you still believe in the tooth mouse too. They use each other all the time and those big fuckin' companies from the North use 'em both. The whole country's a swamp of grubby deals. They all smell as bad as him, man, from the grunts right up to *los generales*.

ANGELA: Cut it out, Sergeant. Just cut it out.

RÓMULO: Maybe they've got our welfare close to their hearts. Tell you what, but. No-one's taken *their* phones away.

ANGELA: He won't get away with it this time. He's done it before. For ten years / he's run rings around them.

EL TICHO: / Fifteen, but who's counting—

ANGELA: This time, it would bring down the president.

RÓMULO: Reckon the president calls the shots, man?

ANGELA: The *North* wants to extradite him!

RÓMULO: The North. Gimme a break. A tunnel's got two ends, Boss. Who you think buys that shit? I'm not riskin' my life 'coz some acne-faced kid don't know how to keep his nose clean—

ANGELA: We do our job, Sergeant. That's all there is to it.

RÓMULO: We're stuck here like lab rats, man. Know what happens next? We're *dissected*. Listen, let's just get out— [*Quickly glancing at the clock*] Now's the time, man, before this thing blows up right in our fuckin' faces. C'mon I mean it, leave him and go, right now, walk through that door— *hasta luego*. Waddya say?

ANGELA: Sergeant, you're in my bad books already. Don't make it worse or you'll be facing a court martial.

RÓMULO: Getting into *trouble*—figure I give a rat's arse about that? We're already in trouble! You think things can't get worse? Things can get a *shitload* worse! Ask him: he can fuck us up. His gang can fuck us up. The army can fuck us up. The politicians in the capital can fuck us up. You reckon Jesus'll save you? For all I know he's up there waiting his turn like the rest of them.

ANGELA: I mean it, Sergeant. A court martial.

RÓMULO: Please, Angela. Let me pick up my kid before it's too late. *Te lo ruego*—

He reaches out to touch her and she pulls away.

ANGELA: It's Lieutenant Bassols to you, Sergeant. And I'm sure your daughter will just love seeing her papa all dressed in orange, one hour a week for the next twenty-five years.

RÓMULO: So—what? 'Trust in God' like they put on the sides of the cop cars? I'm not a believer.

ANGELA: In God.

RÓMULO: In trust.

ANGELA: I am not about to desert my post, Sergeant.

RÓMULO: Man, general's daughter, the army sure did a number on you, eh Lieutenant? Well, know what they say? Better to run, before you're scalped.

ANGELA: Is that what they say?

RÓMULO: Yes, didn't your papa tell you?

ANGELA *bites her tongue.* RÓMULO *drinks a glass of water.*

ANGELA: [*interior voice*] *No, not papa. He got it backwards. First he was scalped, and then he ran. Left us to bury him and cry over him. Left me to face the photographers' flash and the stares and the whispers and the sniggers at school. Hiding under the covers all day and crying myself to sleep. We lost everything, papa. Everything but our honour. The one thing of yours I kept.*

[*Out loud*] This conversation is over, Sergeant García. Just man up and listen to me. If the worst really does come to the worst—

RÓMULO: Oh, holy fuck.

ANGELA: At least we can make sure we've covered all the bases. Did you check out the fire escapes?

RÓMULO: Didn't see.

ANGELA: Oh, but moths you see fine. Truth is, I may as well be here all by myself.

RÓMULO: Whatever.

ANGELA: No, Sergeant. Not whatever. Not whenever. Now. We were told to secure the perimeter. Where are the fire exits? There could be someone out there already. We don't know. We've got to find out.

RÓMULO: Okay, no need to bust my balls about it. I'll go.

ANGELA: No, no, Sergeant, I don't think that's such a good idea, do you? *I'll* go. You just stay put and guard the suspect. Think you can handle that?

RÓMULO: Yes, *sir*.

ANGELA *starts to leave the room.*

ANGELA: Don't touch the suspect, Sergeant.

RÓMULO: Sure thing, Boss.

ANGELA: That's an order, Sergeant. So help me God, if I had a second set of handcuffs—

RÓMULO: Okay, okay, I get the picture.

ANGELA: Don't even speak to him.

RÓMULO: I'll be silent as an egg, Lieutenant.

ANGELA *exits. Silence.*

EL TICHO: An egg? I thought birds chirped away inside their shells.

Awkward silence. RÓMULO *takes out a cigarette.* EL TICHO *points at the 'No Smoking' sign.* RÓMULO *stares at him in disbelief, then puts it back, sits down next to* EL TICHO.

RÓMULO: Some birds sing, some birds don't.

EL TICHO: So now you know who I am, boy.

Another awkward silence, until ROMULO *cracks.*

RÓMULO: Look, I'm no good with faces, *señor*. I get a haircut, I scare myself in the mirror.

EL TICHO: Is that a fact? Perhaps the police force is not for you … [*Looking at the tattoo*] I see you have dreams, egg-man. [*Interior voice*] *Said the hawk to the robin.*

RÓMULO: Yeah, when I was a kid, I was gonna be a *matador* too. [*Interior voice*] *Said the bullfighter to the bull.*

EL TICHO: When I was young, I too had dreams.

RÓMULO: Reckon you're about the most famous man in the world, yeah? They write *corridos* about you, man.
[*Singing*] I like to walk in the mountains
I grew up in the bush

EL TICHO and RÓMULO: [*singing together*] Where I learnt maths
Just by counting sacks.

EL TICHO: [*singing*] I like to get away from the nets
Cast by the feds.*

---

* See *'Pacas De A Kilo'*, by Teodoro Bello:
https://www.youtube.com/watch?v=NBvMXqNBzu8

RÓMULO: Now you're on all the wanted posters—north *and* south of the border.

EL TICHO: Better to stay cool than pack heat, son. Like the feathered snake. He slithers in the long grass where no-one sees him, and suddenly …

He leans close to RÓMULO, *then claps his hands loudly.*

He strikes.

RÓMULO: That's not how I remember / that story.

EL TICHO: [*pointing to the tattoo*] Is that him?

RÓMULO: Nah … He's no snake in the grass, man. He *soars* on / the wind.

EL TICHO: Suit yourself. I prefer land to air.

RÓMULO: Some of us don't have the choice.

EL TICHO: I can see you're a family man. Your superior—

RÓMULO: Not her.

EL TICHO: I thought as much.

RÓMULO: Know what? She's General Bassols' daughter. You remember—it was all over the news, man. Caught with his fingers in the honey. Came to a sticky end, man.

He mimes shooting himself.

EL TICHO: Ah well, that explains it. I also am a family man. It's a tough job, son.

RÓMULO: Guess so.

EL TICHO: Sometimes you must take hard decisions. To keep them safe.

RÓMULO: [*glancing at the clock*] Oh fuck—

EL TICHO: [*following his gaze*] You are time poor—

RÓMULO: Cash poor too, man—

EL TICHO: Enough of one buys you the other—

RÓMULO: Fuckin' *poor* poor.

EL TICHO: Don't tell me you live off your salary. A policeman who lives off his salary. Well, well—

RÓMULO: Yeah, thanks for the performance review / but—

EL TICHO: With a little help you could spread your wings and fly, birdman.

RÓMULO: Wait—the briefcase? A guy in nothing but his underpants is gonna need cash, for sure. How much, man?

EL TICHO: Go fetch it, son, and then we'll talk.

RÓMULO: A million? *Two* million—?

EL TICHO: I don't concern myself with details—

RÓMULO: Cash? *Gold?*

EL TICHO: Look at me, my friend. I can fix your life forever.

A silence while this sinks in.

RÓMULO: Wait—let me think. Let me think.

EL TICHO: *¡Tu puta madre!* Are you going to use that cock of yours for once or wank off your whole life?

RÓMULO *starts edging towards the door.*

Son. Word of advice. You have a family to think of. A child, let us say. This is no time to be a snake. Or a bird for that matter. *¿Está claro?*

ANGELA *enters.*

ANGELA: What's going on here? I thought I told you not to move.

RÓMULO: Jeez, can't a guy stretch his legs / without filling in a form—?

ANGELA: Stretch your legs on your own time, Sergeant—

RÓMULO: Did you find us an exit strategy?

ANGELA: You and I don't have an *exit strategy*, Sergeant. [*Moving to the bathroom*] Fire escape! Death trap more like. Only thing holding those stairs together are spider webs. No-one's going to risk their neck coming up that way, but I secured them just to be on the safe side.

She exits to the bathroom. We hear a tap running. RÓMULO *exchanges a final look with* EL TICHO *and sneaks out.*

[*Offstage*] You know, I don't think this place has been up to code for ten years. More.

[*Re-entering*] And as for you—*señor.* What did I say about talking to my sergeant?

EL TICHO: To who, sweetheart?

ANGELA: [*standing in the middle of the room, aghast*] Sergeant? [*Running to the door*] Sergeant García, come back! Don't be an idiot! Rómulo! *Rómulo!*

For a moment she seems torn between chasing him or staying, then slams the door shut.

Indio ladino.

Blackout.

SCENE THREE: TEMPTATION

A spotlight on EL TICHO.

EL TICHO: Make no mistake, my business is not a *commodity*. Dreams and escape, that's what I sell: the rich love it and the poor can't get by without it. An excellent business model, you could say—recession proof. But in the North, they hate me for it. For giving them what they want. Forgiving them what they need. They like their dreams, up there in the North, but they prefer to keep their eyes closed. If I'm forced into the light of day, they'll hunt me down and they'll string me up.

My escape—this time, no fucking drug is no fucking use. It's not my dreams that'll do the trick. It's theirs. We all have them, it's like a fat worm, you just have to know how to dig.

A spotlight on RÓMULO.

RÓMULO: A full belly, a woman in my bed, a few beers on Saturday night. It's all I ever wanted, man. Guess two outta three ain't bad, am I right? 'Cept now I've got a kid, and nothin' adds up the same. *No mames*. I didn't see that coming. Reckon I'm nothin' but a useless *cholo* after all. Nothin' special to look at. No family, no money. Went to school but it didn't take. But my little girl, I fuckin' love her, man. And she loves me back; least that's what I figure.

He takes a picture out of his wallet.

Here. Cute, huh. Past her bedtime now. I shoulda been there to read her a story, you know? Or make one up; make her laugh. That's somethin', yeah? It's all I've got to offer, but it's not nothin', am I right?

No such luck, man. *La jefa*, blind as a fucking mole, man, blind as fucking justice. She thinks we've got the devil in a cage. Well, guess what. We're right in there with him.

Lieutenant going on at me 'bout law and duty and all that crap, curdling my milk every fuckin' day. Shit, law and duty, it's pissin' on a wildfire, that's all it is. Know what counts in the North, man? Power and profits. That 'n' holdin' the rest of us way down, make sure we don't get no ideas, shoot a few lousy *indios* every now and then just to stay in practice. Talk about the law all ya want, one way or another it's always brown folk end up screwed.

You want me to play toy soldiers? You want me to take the fucking fall? Like the North gives a fuckin' *pimiento* 'bout my life or my kid's. They'll smoke her childhood. They'll inject her tears. They'll shove her blood up their noses. That's how it is, man, that's how the whole world is. What can I do 'cept tell her a story, make her laugh a bit? It's nothin', man, but what else I got?

A spotlight on ANGELA.

ANGELA: Being a woman in this world takes guts. Ask anyone. Pitiless and cruel. Well, you want tough, try being a cop. A woman guarding the law. That's as tough as it gets. Take no bribes. Crack no jokes. Make no mistakes. But more than that; you need to have faith in it, against all the odds. That's the hard part. It takes courage. Not everyone is up to it, that's God's truth, I'm not afraid to say so. My father—he gave up everything he stood for, for a plate of lentils. His weakness, his stupid weakness, taught me what it means to be strong; how to put sacrifice and duty first every day of my life. It was his last, burnt offering to me.

Faith comes from faith. I'm not so keen on all that nonsense about turning the other cheek, but time after time, Sunday after Sunday—the feeling of some power way above me. I love to raise my voice with others, everyone on the same page, singing to the glory of the Lord. The law is just like that, believe it or not. There is a beautiful harmony that comes out of it, a beautiful eternal order. Sound as a bell.

You just have to know how to hear it. Most people don't. They're too lost in their own little noise. Truth is, that's why we need the police, proper police, to make people listen—like it or not. Poor Rómulo, what does he know, a man like that—born with a tin ear. He's tone deaf to the law. Even when he talks about his daughter, he sounds just like a child himself. He doesn't understand that only order and discipline can save her, can save this whole place. Not silly sentimental old stories. What a waste of time.

I can't say I enjoy having to be the grown up all the time. Never mind. I'm used to it by now. A woman—guarding the law. I'll do what I have to. Even if I have to raise my voice from time to time.

Lights up.

EL TICHO: Alone at last.

ANGELA: Stay away from me.

EL TICHO: Gladly, *señora*, but easier said than done. You see, you are the zookeeper and I am just a humble lion.

ANGELA: Humble nothing. Dear God, this is a disaster. What did you say to him? Did you scare him off? Has he run away?

EL TICHO: [*looking at the clock*] You tell me.

ANGELA: I don't know; I just don't know—Lord Jesus Christ, what have you done?

EL TICHO: I?

ANGELA: Don't play games with *me*, *señor*. It will get you nowhere.

EL TICHO: Oh, I can see that. You have bigger balls. Than your father.

ANGELA: Leave him out of this. Whatever mistakes he made, he paid the price.

EL TICHO: Well, someone did. Do you even shop in the same lovely shops anymore? On the salary of an honest fucking cop?

ANGELA: I don't care about that sort of thing.

EL TICHO: So I see. Look at you. Daughter of the great General Bassols. Handing out speeding tickets on some rat-infested highway in the middle of nowhere. It must make you want to puke.

ANGELA: I'm proud of what I do. I have a reputation to uphold.

EL TICHO: Don't we all.

ANGELA: No, no, *señor*, do not pretend we are cut from the same cloth.

EL TICHO: Correct. I was born with nothing to lose—and you're going to die that way.

ANGELA: Mine comes from knowing right from wrong.

EL TICHO: Oh, who knows what's right and what's wrong / nowadays?

ANGELA: Debating ethics with a mass murderer—

EL TICHO: That's a lie—

ANGELA: Oh, I beg your pardon, I thought we were talking about reputations. Truth is, people trust me. And this uniform? My father would have been proud—

EL TICHO: Bravo! Bravo! A bull's ear for you, *mi pequeña torera*! But I have an ear for bullshit. You're playing to an empty house. Not even your father knows how much hard work it has taken—

ANGELA: I know. And Jesus knows—

EL TICHO: To fall so far. And when you take off that clownish outfit at night? When you strip to the skin and stare in the mirror at what is left of your beauty, what then? Do you still cry? Or do you close all the curtains … take out a photo of dear papa … and stick it full of knives.

ANGELA: You disgust me.

EL TICHO: You should be in the army, not in exile.

ANGELA: I'm enforcing the law. That's good enough for me. God knows we need it around here, *señor*.

EL TICHO: The law? What has the law done for you lately, except destroy your father's life? And ruin yours into the bargain. Poor you. Life on the line, no-one to help, nowhere to turn. You can thank the law for that, too, sweetheart.

ANGELA: *¡Cállate!* I don't want your pity.

EL TICHO: I'm not offering you pity. I'm offering you a way out, my dear. You're in a tight spot. The rules don't cover this—this *situation*. I'm sure your superiors would understand.

ANGELA: The Captain—

EL TICHO: I don't mean the Captain, darling. Time to take it up the line. Isn't that what you believe in? The chain of command—

ANGELA: You think I've got the Commissioner's number? That's not how the system works.

EL TICHO: Just hand me the phone. Then we'll see how the system works. C'mon, my dear, leave it to me. There are rules, of course there are, but sometimes you have to go straight to the top. *Their* job is to see the big picture. You've been carrying around this weight for a long time. Isn't it getting heavy?

ANGELA: We all have our cross to bear, *señor*—

EL TICHO: Just play your cards right, and who knows where it might take you? The honour of a job well done. A commendation. A promotion. A transfer. It's easy when you know how.

ANGELA: You can't be serious.

EL TICHO: Oh, I am deadly serious, my dear.

ANGELA: You're a wanted man, not a—a—senator.

EL TICHO: Do you not see how close those things are? I can do this for you. You could become a *real* officer in a *real* army. A woman with battalions to command. Imagine it, my dear. A second chance.

ANGELA *doesn't respond but her body tightens.*

A second General Bassols.

Another silence.

Call it—*redemption* …

ANGELA: Only God redeems—

EL TICHO: Oh, spare me the sermon! I can see right through you, girl. You and I both know this is what you want in your heart of hearts. I'm your fucking fairy godfather. So hop into the pumpkin, sweetheart, before it's too late. You deserve it. Call it compensation.

He has taken a step too far.

ANGELA: For what—for him—from you? Who do you think I am? I'd rather die.

EL TICHO: Oh, you do disappoint me. You are an orphan in the ways of the world, Lieutenant Bassols. Your father was much the same. He made the wrong choice all those years ago, my dear. He was only a bagman, yes, but if he'd carried mine none of this would have happened.

ANGELA: You speak of papa like he is just a part of history, a statistic, a punch line. But not for me. He was strong and kind. He was my world. And now he's gone.

EL TICHO: So let me give you a piece of fatherly advice—

ANGELA: *Motherfucker.*

EL TICHO: Well. My mother is well away, thank God, but you, little one, are very near. Think what we could do.

ANGELA: [*pointing her gun*] Not part of the job description, *señor*.

EL TICHO: Yet here you are. Facing the music. A law of one.

ANGELA: That's just the weight I have to carry. [*Interior voice*] *The problem with temptation is that it's tempting.*

The door opens. ANGELA *turns, gun raised.* RÓMULO *puts his hands up, holding the briefcase.*

Sergeant!—you're full of surprises today. Forget your passport?

RÓMULO: C'mon, man, think I was doin' a runner?

ANGELA: Certainly felt that way.

RÓMULO: I'm not crazy. It's a deal. We're cutting a deal here.

He puts the briefcase on the table.

ANGELA: Ah, so that's what this is in aid of.

EL TICHO: How's my boy Víctor? Still tethered?

RÓMULO: Still bleating. [*Opening the briefcase*] *¡Ay, cabrón!* See that?—Hey, wait a sec … what's this?

He sits down and starts counting to himself.

ANGELA: Careful, Sergeant. Mind you get the full thirty pieces.

RÓMULO: Just shut up, will ya, I'm trying to count. Fifty thou, give or take.

EL TICHO: Are you sure?

RÓMULO: I put my life at risk for what … a *tip*? 'Here you are, *muchacha*, go buy yourself something pretty.' Think I'm one of your low-life rent boys? / Like you can buy me off with a drop of your cum—?

EL TICHO: Put your rod back in your pants, boy. Unlike you, I never forget a prick—

RÓMULO: Reckon you're *better* than me, huh?

RÓMULO *sits back down and takes several rasping breaths.*

Fuck!

EL TICHO: Listen, son, take a Xanax.

RÓMULO: Fuckin' shit of a day.

EL TICHO: Think of it as a test—

RÓMULO: Well, you fuckin' flunked it, / you—

EL TICHO: A down payment.

RÓMULO: Waddya have in mind?

EL TICHO: You tell me.

ANGELA: This has gone far enough. Banking hours are over—

EL TICHO: Don't be silly, sweetheart. I operate twenty-four-seven.

RÓMULO *glances at the clock.*

RÓMULO: C'mon, Chief, put the gun down why don't you, you're making me nervous. What did you put in that notebook of yours? You didn't—

ANGELA: No. Thought I'd better wait and see—before I did something you'd regret.

RÓMULO: [*speaking aside*] Good. 'Coz this is our lucky day, man.

ANGELA: Really?

RÓMULO: No, listen to me, just *listen*.

ANGELA: You've changed your tune all of a sudden.

RÓMULO: You heard him, man. This is just the tip of the iceberg. He said to me—he said—he can fix my life forever.

ANGELA: When? When did he say that? Didn't I tell you—?

RÓMULO: That's not the point.

ANGELA: Jesus, Rómulo, your *life*'s the point.

RÓMULO: No, it's *his*. How much you reckon it's worth?

ANGELA: I wouldn't give a *centavo* for it.

RÓMULO: Oh, don't you get it? I've been dreaming of this my whole fucking life. A change in the weather. A lucky break for once. A million—more—think what I could do / with that—

ANGELA: It's not worth it—

RÓMULO: Oh, sure, easy for you to say.

ANGELA: You're a policeman, Sergeant. You swore an oath—

RÓMULO: Holy fuckin' chalice, I've sworn plenty of fucking oaths. Figure I give a rat's balls 'bout this crappy job—?

ANGELA: Well, I do—

RÓMULO: 'Course ya do, army brat like you, *la tira*'s in your blood.

ANGELA: You think my family's ever been a *plus* for me?

RÓMULO: You do alright—

ANGELA: Do I?

RÓMULO: Reckon I samba off to work humming the / national anthem—?

ANGELA: I do it / the hard way—

RÓMULO: *La tira*, man—it's a bit of cash and / it comes with a gun—

ANGELA: Living it down—

RÓMULO: So you don't get pushed around—

ANGELA: Starting from scratch—

RÓMULO: Fringe benefit every now and then, know what I'm sayin'? It's not worth dying for, man—

ANGELA: That's what I'm trying / to tell you.

RÓMULO: I've never had nothing— *nada*, not even a pair of boots don't nag my feet all day. His money, man. It's a new start—for my kid— far from here—safe, you know? I wanna give her a chance. What *chance* I ever have? Work for peanuts in some bullshit factory—risk my life every day for the *narcos*?—like the guys I hung out with, see?

ANGELA: Yes and they're probably all dead by now—

EL TICHO: I've always loved coming of age stories with a moral, but I'm on a tight schedule. [*Stealing a glance at the clock*] Do we have a deal or don't we? My competitors are easier to deal with than you.

RÓMULO: Some died, yeah. Not me. I'm a survivor, man. But I'm tired of fuckin' *surviving*. You want to get on, you need money.

You wanna play the Immaculate Virgin Cop—well, guess what. You need money for that too, man. Reckon we all need money. You wanna look a gift horse up the blowhole, be my fuckin' guest. All the more for me.

ANGELA: This is insane! I won't cover for you—

Feeling for their guns, they stand and circle one another.

RÓMULO: Big surprise, man—

ANGELA: I'll tell the truth.

RÓMULO: Oh, like you're not going to run off and sell your story to the highest bidder?

ANGELA: Maybe I'll tell them the truth too.

RÓMULO: *Jefa*, why do you always have to make everything so fuckin' difficult? Tell ya what, but, I got another old saying for you. *Los muertos no hablan.*

ANGELA: If all they find is my body—you think you'll get away with it?

RÓMULO *pushes* ANGELA *against the wall, shoving his rifle up against her neck.*

RÓMULO: What gives you the right to stand in my fucking way? Jesus Christ? Daddy? Ya pearly white skin?

ANGELA: [*whispering*] Truth is, Sergeant, your ex got it right. You can't be trusted.

He shoves her to the ground and points his rifle at her.

{ RÓMULO: Bullshit. Bullshit—
{ EL TICHO: You let her talk to you like that—?

RÓMULO: No-one gives me a break, man. You and the whole mother-fucking lot of 'em.

ANGELA: Rómulo, for Jesus' sake, you think you can just grab the money and—what? Cross the border and evaporate?

RÓMULO: No, not the fucking North. / Better than that—

ANGELA: You'll spend the rest of your life on the run—

RÓMULO: I'll take my chances.

ANGELA: The North will come after you. You'll be the pin-up boy for law enforcement agencies you can't even spell. How long before your crummy luck runs out and they track you down? If the cartels don't get you first.

RÓMULO: I don't care what happens to me anymore.

EL TICHO: What are you waiting / for?—

ANGELA: Elisa? This is for *Elisa*? Jesus, / Rómulo—

RÓMULO: [*looking alarmed at* EL TICHO] Shut up, shut up, shut up why don't you?

EL TICHO: Oh, for fuck's sake, do it or don't do it but stop *talking* about it, / you useless faggot.

ANGELA: [*starting to stand up*] You take his money and then what? *His* enemies will be *her* enemies. She'll spend the rest of her life looking over her shoulder. Is that what you mean by freedom? Call that a lucky break? Jesus wept, Rómulo, you're a man: I guess the obvious just doesn't occur to you. You think these *narcos* play nice—?

EL TICHO: Just shut her fuckin' mouth—

ANGELA: They want to get him, who do you think they go after? Go ahead—ask him. Ask him how many of his girlfriends are rotting in jail, paying for his crimes. Ask him how many are dead.

> EL TICHO *'s expression has turned to obsidian.*

Women—we're nothing round here. We're spent like cash, we're sent like letters, we're thrown away like used tissues. Left by the side of the road or taken out with the trash and nobody looks twice. You, you get a tattoo to show how *macho* / you are—But men like him—they carve their tattoos / so deep into our flesh—

RÓMULO: Okay, okay. / Stop it. Please—

ANGELA: We bleed out. Do what you have to do. Flap off like that bird of yours; just don't say you're doing it for her. You might fool yourself, but you can't fool me.

RÓMULO: [*lowering his rifle*] I'll never see her / again—

ANGELA: [*energised*] There's not a moment to lose.

> *For the first time,* EL TICHO *shows anxiety. He follows her gaze and tugs at his handcuffs.*

RÓMULO: Yeah? You got a better plan?

ANGELA: Certainly. We kill him.

> *Blackout.*

SCENE FOUR: JUDGING THE DEVIL

A spotlight on ANGELA.

ANGELA: El Altiplano. The highlands. Our lifeline to the North. Where I was born. Where I was raised. A decent place with decent God-fearing people. But back then; truth is, nowhere was safe. The cartels were taking pot shots at each other willy-nilly. There'd be a spittle of gunfire in the middle of the night, and you'd throw yourself under the bed without thinking. Without even waking up. You did what you had to do—to stay alive.

Anyway. That day. Lunch hour—the streets were packed. All of a sudden, a boy on the back of a *moto* throws a grenade right at the feet of, I don't know, some pimply dealer stuck on the wrong end of a turf war. Honestly, they were just teenagers, the both of them, didn't know better and couldn't care less. For a second everyone freezes like they're getting their photo taken, and then it goes off. Loudest sound I ever heard. Broken glass falling like snow. Smoke everywhere, I can't see through the haze too well. Can't hear much either, my ears are ringing from the noise. People running, hiding behind rubbish bins, shooting at each other. One moment it was an arcade, the next it's a war zone. There's a guy in an expensive suit on the other side of the street and he's running but he's got all these fancy shopping bags and he keeps tripping over them, and I think to myself, *¡Ponte buzo!* Watch out, dipstick.

I throw myself on the ground and try not to move—I'm shaking like a leaf, praying too. That's when I see her, this child, she's tottering across the road, bullets and smoke everywhere. I don't know, maybe she's three or four, pretty white dress with cherries on it. I remember the dress distinctly. She's just walking and crying. I shout out to her to get down. *¡Abajo, abajo!* She's right in front of me, wandering around like she's lost.

So I grab her and I pull her down. To get her out the way. *Abajo, abajo.* Suddenly, I hear something. A whizzing, whining, shrieking sound. Fast. Loud. Right in my ear. Then everything goes completely still. She doesn't move, she doesn't cry. It's her. Dead. The End.

A spotlight on EL TICHO.

EL TICHO: The end? I don't give it a thought. Why should I? The brighter the candle, the faster it burns. Dying is easy, anyone can do it. Killing is harder than you suppose. But here is my advice, if you permit me. If you want to do it, you better do it right. Because if you don't, you've stirred up a very angry fucking wasp I can tell you. And he may be better at it than you.

Lights up.

ANGELA: This day has been a long time coming.

RÓMULO: This day has been a long time *going*.

ANGELA: 'Do you know who I am,' he said. Now I know. He's *Satan*—

{ RÓMULO: / *Say what?*

{ EL TICHO: *What*—?

ANGELA: I leave him with you for two minutes and look what happens. You were going to *kill* me, Rómulo.

RÓMULO: No! Angela—I wouldn't—

ANGELA: You were, you were. He spun you a fairytale and you fell for it—

RÓMULO: I saw red, man.

ANGELA: Neck and heels—

RÓMULO: What you said, man—

ANGELA: Oh, Rómulo, you're easy meat / for someone like him—

RÓMULO: My girl—*my* girl—

ANGELA: We all are.

RÓMULO: To keep her—to keep her safe—

He struggles to explain himself.

ANGELA: Safe? We're none of us safe, Rómulo. Headless corpses hanging from lampposts. Bodies rotting in the gutter.

EL TICHO: You spend too much time on the internet—

ANGELA: No, I spend too much time on the *highway*.

RÓMULO: *Jefa*, c'mon man—

ANGELA: My papa is *dead* because of you—

EL TICHO: I'm hardly to blame for the greed / of others.

ANGELA: That's how you make your money—

EL TICHO: Don't blame me for your so-called drug war, sweetheart.

I'm just a middleman, between the producers and the consumers. Blame geography.

ANGELA: Oh, sure, the North, our favourite alibi. Well, they believe in action, not excuses in the North.

RÓMULO: They believe in getting their own fuckin' way in the North, that's for sure.

EL TICHO: [*interior voice*] *None of you knows the North like I do. In the North, everything comes at a price. The question is, are you prepared to pay?*

He looks at the clock.

RÓMULO: I'm burning up here. I can't breathe. I'm gonna try and cool off. Okay—? Lieutenant—?

ANGELA: *Dios mío*. It's time someone put a stop to it—

RÓMULO: Maybe you should too.

ANGELA: [*to* EL TICHO] Truth is, we'd be better off without you—

RÓMULO: [*exiting to the bathroom*] We'd be the same / without him, man—

EL TICHO: Not so, I am a peacemaker. Blessed are the peacemakers, isn't that what it says?

ANGELA: Peace? You call this peace? Hundreds of thousands of victims.

EL TICHO: You prefer my competitors? I'm a practical man. I kill if I must. But the younger generation, these so-called young bloods. Blood is their pleasure, their trip. Spoiled brats, the lot of them. Believe me, they need a father's firm hand to keep them in line. Get rid of me and then you will know hell. And for what? Because my business model offends you.

ANGELA: It's business for you maybe.

EL TICHO: We're both in the same business, sweetheart. The snow business. What did you say?—like a soft white powder that hides the dirt—

ANGELA: Shut up!

She snatches RÓMULO's paliacate *from the back of the chair.*

EL TICHO: God, coke. Snort what you please. *Tengo*—

ANGELA *gags* EL TICHO *with her usual precise actions.*

RÓMULO: [*re-entering without his rifle*] Oh c'mon, man, that was my lucky hanky!

ANGELA: Don't you see? It's not luck, it's God's will he's here—after all this time.

RÓMULO: Mother of God. I thought *I* was the bad cop. Serve and protect; law and order. That's your line—remember?

ANGELA: Don't you see? He was right. He was right all along.

RÓMULO: What happened to those precious rules you're such a pain in the fuckin' clacka about?

ANGELA: He said it—sometimes the rules are not enough. Sometimes God gives you an opportunity to lead the way. To be strong, to take a stand. A higher law.

RÓMULO: Jesus Christ, Chief, under my plan, we ended up with a cool million, and his enemies were our enemies. Under your plan, his enemies are still our enemies, his friends are our enemies, and no-one gets a million. Man, that deal's worse than free trade.

ANGELA: It's all about making a deal for you, isn't it?

RÓMULO: You won't get away with it, / man—

ANGELA: I don't intend to get away with it. I'll pay the price. That's why I'm different from him and his kind.

RÓMULO: Kind? What kind? Whose kind am I, Lieutenant? Am I his kind too? Just another shifty little brown *indio*?

ANGELA: That's not what I'm talking about—

RÓMULO: It never fucking is. Know what they call you down at the station but?

ANGELA: I'd rather not—

RÓMULO: Snow White. You're too high and mighty for your own fucking good, Snow White. '*No sea igualado*,' shit. Round here, man, we're all his kind, more or less—

> ANGELA *takes out her gun and moves to* EL TICHO. RÓMULO *feels for his rifle.*

¡*Mierda!*

> *He steps between* ANGELA *and* EL TICHO.

ANGELA: Someone's got to be strong enough to get this country back on the right path.

RÓMULO: Oh, and it's always gotta be *you*, eh, Snow White? Only this time, we'll all pay the price—saint, devil, and innocent fucking bystander. *Santa Muerte*, I can see the fucking feel-good headlines already. Martyred cop slays drug lord. Page one, man, you'll be front-page news. Luckless fucking sidekick caught in crossfire, see page twenty-six. Fuck.

ANGELA: Jesus will show me the way.

RÓMULO: Yeah? I went to one of those mad services of yours, remember? Reckon once'll do me. All those *locas* moaning and waving their arms around like they're being boned by the sacred dildo of Christ. I'm coming, Lord, I'm coming!

> ANGELA *swiftly trips* RÓMULO, *who falls. Then she puts the gun to* EL TICHO*'s head.*

ANGELA: Enough! This place is a web of lies and death, and you, *señor*, are the spider who sits in the heart of it. You're a traitor to the land I grew up in.

RÓMULO: Angela. *Stop.*

ANGELA: I know what I'm doing.

RÓMULO: Oh, oh, man, now I know what this is about—how stupid of me not to see it before. Reckon you always know best, don't you?

ANGELA: This time I do.

RÓMULO: Tell ya what, Boss, maybe Jesus whispers sweet nothings in your ear, but you can be a bit hard of fuckin' hearing, don't ya reckon?

ANGELA: What?

RÓMULO: Yeah, if you hadn't pulled that poor kid down in front of you? What then, huh? Who'd be dead now, man?

ANGELA: No, that's not true. That's not true. That's not how it was.

RÓMULO: You tried to save her life? Don't make me laugh. She saved *yours*.

ANGELA: It *wasn't* like that—

RÓMULO: Reckon you can stop the pain, Angela? By killing him? Reckon you can rewind the clock?

ANGELA: It *wasn't* my fault.

RÓMULO: Say what you like 'bout General Bassols, least he fessed up.

ANGELA: It wasn't. It wasn't—

> ANGELA *tears the gag off* EL TICHO, *but she is uncertain, weeping.*

EL TICHO: Your little faggot friend gets it, darling. You and I have more in common than you think. *C'mon,* pull the trigger, bitch.

ANGELA: *¡Abajo, abajo!*

> *At the last moment she pulls the gun away from* EL TICHO *and*

shoots. He cries out in pain, holding his ear. RÓMULO *is also shaken, close to tears.*

RÓMULO: Fuck. I gotta take a piss.

He exits to bathroom.

Blackout.

SCENE FIVE: THE QUETZAL

A spotlight on RÓMULO.

RÓMULO: Guys like the old man, they go by many names. *Pepenadores, buzos, chatarreros.* Seagulls scrounging on a sea of garbage, see? Back in the day, that's how he made a few lousy bucks, picking through the scraps the filthy rich chuck out. You rich, you filthy, know what I'm sayin'?

Nothin' but a shantytown—old bits of wood and tin and cardboard thrown together any which way, you know how they say, the holes in the roof—too small to let the sun in and too big to keep the rain out. Good thing, man, sure you get wet but least you can drink it, otherwise what was there 'cept the slops in the streets that everybody pisses and shits in already. But folks born there, folks die. No-one buried there, that's for fucking sure, they just sink down into the muck till it covers 'em like a tide. Cold nights, the *pepenadores* get a big old drum and burn whatever they can find for heat, and the smoke rises into the sky, and the stink and sparks drift over us till I'd gag on the fuckin' fumes. Breathed it in, coughed it up. The old man'd come home, smelling like stale shit and flat beer or flat shit and stale beer, I don't know, and someone even shittier than him would have to sponge him down [*gesturing: the connection to Scene One should be apparent*] and fuckin' watch out, case you look him in the eyes and get whacked for your trouble. Someone like me, see?

Long gone. Shopping malls and shi-shi apartments now. Cheapest land in the city, man, some developer snapped it up for a song, made a packet for sure. Money, friends, money, am I right? They call it Hope Towers. Good one, man. Sick fuckin' joke I reckon. It's the poor need hope, but only the rich can fuckin' afford it.

Lights up. ROMULO *returns with his rifle.*

So. Was it good for you, too?

ANGELA: I couldn't do it.

RÓMULO: Tell ya what, buddy, next time Jesus shares his plans for saving the fuckin' world, keep them to your fuckin' self.

ANGELA: This will be my punishment for being weak.

RÓMULO: Shit. What a mess, what a fucking mess. Give me your lousy gun before you waste any more fucking bullets on the furniture.

ANGELA: I thought Jesus would show me the way, but he said nothing, nothing.

RÓMULO: Yeah, he's good at that, man. Gimme the gun.

ANGELA: An officer shall not surrender his firearm …

RÓMULO: Hey, Angela! A bit late to be quoting fuckin' regulations at me, wouldn't ya say?

> ANGELA *pushes her gun away.* RÓMULO *puts it in his jacket pocket.*

I'd bin that fuckin' notebook of yours too, if I was you, 'coz if it comes to comparing diaries—

ANGELA: Rómulo—

RÓMULO: Shut up, shut up, let me think / willya—?

> EL TICHO *has gradually been recovering.*

EL TICHO: Haven't you done enough?

ANGELA: I'm cold.

EL TICHO: You think I'm talking to you, you mad God-bothering cunt? *La puta madre*, I thought you were deluded you went into politics, not the fucking highway patrol.

ANGELA: Cold.

RÓMULO: You're in shock. We all are, man.—

> RÓMULO *takes the small white blanket from the end of the bed and drapes it over her in a surprisingly tender gesture.*

EL TICHO: You mothers' whores, I am out of patience. You should be in therapy, the both of you, instead of roaming the highways, putting the lives of innocent fucking motorists at risk.

RÓMULO: Hey! I'm in charge here.

EL TICHO: Who do you think you're fucking kidding, boy—you've never been in charge of a thing. Come here. I want a word with you.

RÓMULO: [*sitting down anxiously*] Mind if—mind if I smoke?

EL TICHO: I'm not the one killing myself.

RÓMULO: Dyin' quickly or dyin' slowly, what's it matter?

EL TICHO: As they say, if you're born to be hanged, you'll never be drowned.

> ANGELA *sits apart, lost in her own thoughts, while* RÓMULO *and* EL TICHO *talk together.*

RÓMULO: Yeah, fuckin' got that right, man. When you were growing up, did you think it'd end like this?

ANGELA: [*interior voice*] *I just want to go home, papa. Lie down with the snow at my back and the sun on my face.*

EL TICHO: Actually, it's better than I expected.

ANGELA: [*interior voice*] *And the blinding light, bright from another world. Melting me right into the snow.*

RÓMULO: Yeah … Me too, man.

> *His leg is shaking.*

ANGELA: [*interior voice*] *Until there's nothing of me left at all. Till I can't tell where I stop and the snow begins.*

EL TICHO: You are a jumping bean, my friend.

RÓMULO: Say what?

EL TICHO: Those little beans. You know them? They have baby moths trapped inside them. Put them in a pan and heat them up, they start to cook. The moths, they try and get away. They have no brains, they are just tiny insects, still, they know enough to try and get away from the fire. But they're trapped inside the beans. Hotter and hotter it gets. So the beans start jumping. Jumping like crazy.

ANGELA: [*interior voice*] *Was that it, papa? Did you blind yourself in the light too—?*

RÓMULO: Yeah?

EL TICHO: Look, boy. Any minute, my men are going to come storming through that door. They're not going to knock— *room service.* You think you can stop them? You and that flightless hairy-winged angel of the ever-fucking Lord?

> RÓMULO *starts shaking again.*

You want to get out of here alive? You wish to see that girl of yours again?

ANGELA: [*interior voice*] *Was it like that, papa?*

EL TICHO: Do you—?

RÓMULO: It's too late. It's over. It's over.

EL TICHO: [*looking at the clock*] Time to stop jumping, son.

ANGELA: [*interior voice*] *Everything dissolving in the glare of light?*

RÓMULO: Tell me what to do. I don't know anymore.

ANGELA: [*interior voice*] *The brightness and the coldness and the surrender to—to—*

EL TICHO: You can begin by taking these damn sex toys off me—

RÓMULO *approaches* ANGELA.

ANGELA: [*interior voice:*] *To nothing at all ...*

RÓMULO *cautiously removes the keys from her vest pocket.*

EL TICHO: Give me back my phone.

RÓMULO *moves to pick up the phone.*

ANGELA: [*interior voice*] *Did you think you heard it? Saw it?*

EL TICHO: Take the briefcase. I never saw it, I never saw you—

ANGELA: [*interior voice*] *When there was nothing there ...*

RÓMULO: No way, just leave me and my kid out of it, right?

ANGELA: [*interior voice*] *Nothing but nothing at all ...*

EL TICHO: Keys.

ANGELA: [*interior voice*] *Oh, papa, I'm so sorry ...*

RÓMULO *begins to move.*

[*Interior voice*] *So* sorry *for you—*

EL TICHO: And one last thing. A security you can be trusted.

There is a stunned, horrified silence from RÓMULO.

Are you a little slow on the uptake, *muchacho*?

RÓMULO: Oh no, no—

EL TICHO: I heard you mumbling about *La Santa Muerte*. You are correct, son. The black witch will expect to be paid tonight. Ah, but who will it be?—that's where you come in.

RÓMULO: I couldn't—I—I—

EL TICHO: The girl. Elisa. You would sacrifice her for this cow—?

ANGELA: [*suddenly fully present*] Don't fall for it, Rómulo.

EL TICHO: Ah, Angela—

RÓMULO: I need air. I can breathe out, but I can't breathe in.

> *He moves to the air con.*

EL TICHO: Pity is wasted on the pitiful, boy.

> RÓMULO *struggles with the air con. He talks to himself and the air con during the following exchange.* EL TICHO *and* ANGELA *pay no attention to him.*

ANGELA: Is this how you get your kicks? Playing God?

EL TICHO: Does it look to you like I'm playing?

RÓMULO: I can't decide who lives or dies. / No-one should—

ANGELA: Ruining lives—

EL TICHO: All I do is defend myself. / I start no trouble—

ANGELA: Your mother must be ashamed / of you—

RÓMULO: It's not *fair*—!

EL TICHO: You bitch, you shut your fuckin' hole. Everything I've done, I've done for family. For *her*.

RÓMULO: Sure as fuck / I don't need no crystal ball to tell me how this story ends—

ANGELA: For your *mother* you rape and murder—?

EL TICHO: Another shitty Northern lie. I've built schools, hospitals. What about you?

ANGELA: I haven't slaughtered thousands / of people—

RÓMULO: Know what? It always ends the same, guys like me getting hung out / to fuckin' dry—

EL TICHO: Listen, sweetheart, in these parts you and your kind hunt me down like a cougar. But where I am from. Where the light of your great nation doesn't shine. There, they *pray* to me.

ANGELA: They're scared to death of you, / you mean.

RÓMULO: It makes me want / to throw up—

EL TICHO: Love, fear, who can say? There's always a hint of chilli in / the beans—

RÓMULO: You know? You know—?

ANGELA: How many children have you killed?

EL TICHO: Never have I done that.

ANGELA: [*gesturing to* RÓMULO, *but completely focused on* EL TICHO]

No, you get some other poor sap to do it / for you—

RÓMULO *is still struggling with the air con.*

RÓMULO: Fucking shit of a— / shit of a—nothing—fucking—*works*—

EL TICHO: [*gesturing to* RÓMULO, *but completely focused on* ANGELA]
Tell you what, son. Give her back her gun and maybe she'll blow
her brains out, save us all the trouble. The apple never falls far from
the tree / they say—

RÓMULO: [*shooting repeatedly at the air con*] *Shut the fuck up!*

Shocked silence.

ANGELA: Rómulo—you could hurt somebody—!

RÓMULO: [*returning to the main conversation*] No-one ever listens to
people like me until we start shooting—!

ANGELA: Think about your daughter.

RÓMULO: Man, I am so *fucking* sick of being told what to think. Every
day of my life, someone has told me what to do. You, *boy*, take a
number, wait in line, do what you're told. Now I go back to Hope
Towers and I can't even get a fucking drink in their fancy fucking
taquería. Even my money's the wrong colour, I reckon. *Hey, dude*,
I say, *don't you know who I am?* And they don't, Bassols. They do
not have a fucking clue.

ANGELA: Rómulo—

RÓMULO: You know, man, you've been thinking about my kid; but I've
been thinking 'bout you.

ANGELA: What?

RÓMULO: So tell me, Lieutenant. When you used her name—in front
of our good friend here—were you really so worried about her? Or
were you already planning on making martyrs of us all?

EL TICHO: Ah, there's a thought.

RÓMULO: That's not a report you've been scribbling, it's your last
fuckin' will.

ANGELA: Rómulo, you can't think that—

RÓMULO: Guess you don't like it when we ignorant brown boys start
thinking for ourselves, right? Reckon poor makes you stupid,
Bassols? I have eyes in my head. I see what's what.

ANGELA: Rómulo, I wouldn't do that to you. / You know that.

RÓMULO: It's not you. It's not *him*. Drug's just the excuse, man, 'coz the real drug is money. I never met anyone who had enough of it—and millions'd kill for it in a heartbeat. It's everywhere, the slums right up against the mansions, the rich hiding behind their razor wire and their big fat wet-lipped security guards. Money buys you violence— violence gets you money. It don't come cheap. It costs. Know what? Reckon it'll cost more and more and more and to hell with the rest of us. To hell with me. To hell with my girl, my bright little girl.

ANGELA: You think he's not like that?

RÓMULO: Man, you just don't get it, lady, do you? This is the endgame. Lock him up or blow his head off, who gives a fuck, someone else will take his place faster than you can say hail Mary—

EL TICHO: Amen to that—!

RÓMULO: [*pointing his gun at* EL TICHO] Shut up, I said—!

EL TICHO: Fuck *you*!

RÓMULO: You think he's some cowboy from the wild west? You think he's from the past? Wake up, man. *He's from the future.* Not just the future of this shithole country: the future of the whole stinking world.

EL TICHO: [*stealing another glance at the clock*] The only future that matters, son, is right around the corner and closing fast.

RÓMULO: That's it, man. I can't slow the future down. I can't change its course. I can't get out of its way. All I can do, man, all I can do is blow it up.

ANGELA: Rómulo, what are you saying?

RÓMULO: [*pointing to his tattoo*] Wanna know what *this* is? You never asked but since I have your undivided fuckin' attention I'll tell you anyway. It's the quetzal, a beautiful bird with wings that shine like emeralds—a god of liberation—

ANGELA: Not my god—

RÓMULO: You don't get to choose your gods, Angela. They choose you. The quetzal was the guardian spirit of our warriors. Then men came from over the seas, dressed not in feathers but in steel.

EL TICHO: *¡Por favor!*—

RÓMULO: The warrior and the quetzal fought hard against them, but a spear shattered the warrior's chest. The quetzal, shrieking with grief, threw herself onto the wound as if she could stop the bleeding, and died there. She'd rather die than live in a cage, see?

ANGELA: It's all a fairytale, Rómulo. It's not true.

RÓMULO: No, listen, man. That's why the quetzal's breast is stained red, as red as blood. That's why it doesn't sing. And never will again, man, never again till one day—when we finally break the chains of this shitty world—

EL TICHO: [*indicating his handcuffs*] Why don't you start with these, you useless motherfucker—?

RÓMULO: The quetzal will sing a *new* song. But for that—we gotta stain our chests with blood. See? We gotta burn this place to ashes and start over. I can't hold a tune, man, you've heard me, but my kid, who knows? Doesn't she deserve to find her own voice, man?

ANGELA: I get it, Rómulo. The song of another world—I get it.

RÓMULO: [*suddenly still*] No, man, you don't. How could you? Know what I can't stand 'bout this bullshit? Givin' in and givin' up— [*Tapping his skull*] It's right in here, man. Where'd *that* fuckin' earworm come from? It don't start with me and it won't end with me. It's passed on from father to son. To daughter. It's handed down like fuckin' pearls.

EL TICHO: So spend a bullet on her, why don't you—?

RÓMULO: Your game, her game, I'm not playing no more. A fresh start. *That*'s what I want, man. Least my kid'll have a chance. What chance she got now—?

EL TICHO: You had yours, son.

RÓMULO: Know what, Mister? I am *not* your fucking son. I am no-one's fucking *boy*. I am *a man* and I will be my own man now or die fucking trying. [*To* ANGELA] Forget the money. Forget the deal. Forget the law. I'm gonna let him go. Let him do his worst.

ANGELA: You can't mean that. I know you love Elisa.

RÓMULO: You don't know the first thing 'bout Elisa and me, lady.

ANGELA: No, but I was a girl once, Rómulo. And my father: *deserted* me. Maybe he thought he was doing the right thing too. Maybe he didn't know any better—but he was *wrong*.

RÓMULO: I'm not like your old man, am I? I can't afford to give her pretty clothes and holiday snaps, can I—?

ANGELA: What good's a few photos when you cry every time it snows—?

RÓMULO: What good's me? I don't want to live in a cage. Like the quetzal—I'm sayin' no. Don't you see? [*Pointing at* EL TICHO] No to him, [*encompassing the converging armies*] no to them, no to the whole fucking fucked-up fucking game.

ANGELA *stands.*

Like that's going to work. Never bluff a bluffer, Bassols.

He walks over to EL TICHO. *He leans the rifle against the bed and kneels to undo the cuff closed around the bed leg.*

Call off your men. You want insurance, here I am. We walk out together. Put a spear through me afterwards, I don't care, but Elisa and Angela live. Your life for theirs, see? [*Glancing at the clock*] We got a deal?

EL TICHO: Whatever you say, *señor.*

ANGELA: I'm not going to let you throw your life away. Not after all this.

EL TICHO: Don't be silly, sweetheart. My people are coming. There's going to be a bloodbath.

ANGELA: *Chinga tu madre.*

She blocks the door.

I'm arresting you both for conspiracy to pervert the course of justice.

RÓMULO: [*turning his back on* EL TICHO] Jesus, Angela … why do you have to make everything so fuckin' *difficult?*

EL TICHO *is still handcuffed, but his legs are now free. He stands and grabs the rifle. He points it at* ANGELA.

Struggling to get Angela's gun out of his pocket, RÓMULO *shouts at* ANGELA.

Run, Elisa, run!

EL TICHO *changes aim and fires a single shot at* RÓMULO, *who is thrown to the ground on his back.* EL TICHO *briefly glances at his rifle, a look of panic clouding his face for an instant, which he tries to conceal with bravado.*

EL TICHO: Strike three.

Blackout.

SCENE SIX: COMING FOR ALL OF US

Blackout.

EL TICHO: A father is a skeleton.

ANGELA: A father is a ghost.

RÓMULO: A father is a boy in clothes too big for him.

EL TICHO: A moon, circling out of reach.

ANGELA: A statue in a garden of weeds.

EL TICHO: A broken gun.

RÓMULO: Dried-up blood on sandy ground.

ANGELA: A snowman, melted in the sun.

RÓMULO and ANGELA: [*together*] A father is a voice that vanishes into silence—

RÓMULO: Only to come back in a child's song.

> *A spotlight on* EL TICHO.

EL TICHO: A father is a curse. What did he ever do but slap us around—? Until I put a stop to it. That was that. It was weak to be so angry. No, correction, it was only weak to show it. Anger is a weapon best concealed.

I prefer not to drag up the past. And perhaps, if a father is any use, it is that he stands like a *calaca* in the middle of the road, with his empty eyes and fleshless bones, so you can't turn back. Now I am a *calaca* for other children. When did I stop being a boy and turn into a curse? When did I get so old? I hardly know, myself. I hardly know myself.

> *Blackout.*

ANGELA: *No!*

> *Lights up.* ANGELA *runs to* RÓMULO. *She picks up the gun in* RÓMULO*'s hand and points it at* EL TICHO *while squatting next to* RÓMULO, *frantically searching for vital signs.*

Rómulo! Rómulo! Stay with me, Rómulo. Elisa, don't you see? She needs you. She wants you. You're her papa.

> *She gently cradles* RÓMULO*'s head.*

EL TICHO: How touching, my dear. I'd shed a tear but why waste water? Slide the gun this way, get the keys and take these shitty bangles off me. Let's go. Now. [*Looking at the clock*] Hurry up! You think a faded parrot and a bumbling warrior can stop me now?

ANGELA: [*pointing her gun at* EL TICHO] Leave him alone! Haven't you done enough?

EL TICHO: I? Not at all. It's the old black witch, my dear, collecting a debt.

ANGELA: He didn't deserve to die.

EL TICHO: No-one dies because they deserve to, sweetheart. They die because they have to—

He takes the phone from the bed without losing eye contact with ANGELA, *quickly glancing at it before throwing it away in disgust.*

We must get to the car. Let's go.

ANGELA: So go.

EL TICHO: Don't play the innocent with me, sweetheart, you're the insurance now. C'mon, it's checkout time. Move. Move faster.

ANGELA: I'm not leaving him.

EL TICHO: He's *dead.*

ANGELA: So who'll take care of him now?

EL TICHO: You stubborn bitch, don't you know when you've lost? Move. Move, move, why don't you?

She pushes RÓMULO*'s head away and stands up, gun still trained on* EL TICHO. *A momentary stand-off. Suddenly,* RÓMULO *sits bolt upright, inhales as if for the first time, his eyes wide.*

RÓMULO: [*wheezing*] Forgot … to reload …

EL TICHO: Oh, for—

He throws the rifle at ANGELA *but she dodges it.*

Okay, that's it, I'm done with you two and your little *telenovela.*

He walks to the door and turns around on the threshold.

Shoot me if you dare: I doubt either of you knows how.

As EL TICHO *walks toward the door,* RÓMULO *struggles to his feet. Both he and* ANGELA *jump him at the last moment.*

RÓMULO: ¡Abajo! ¡Vas p'abajo, cabrón!

EL TICHO *falls to the floor. They overpower him, drag him back and manage to cuff his leg. As* EL TICHO *speaks,* RÓMULO *staggers to the coffee table, and* ANGELA *covers his shoulders with the blanket.*

EL TICHO: [*looking at the clock*] No! No, no, no, no, no. *¿Dónde chingados está mi gente?* You can't trust anything in this country. You can't even trust the *puercos* to take a fuckin' bribe anymore. But you can trust me, you twin cunts. I will take you in the night and I will have you messed up inch by fuckin' inch. Know this. You and your family, you're gonna die! I'm gonna feed you to the fucking cattle. You're all gonna die!

RÓMULO: You got to think of better threats, man. That ship has sailed. We were always gonna die—from the moment we ran into you.

ANGELA: From the day we were born, Rómulo.

> ANGELA *kisses him—perhaps tender, perhaps urgent, but not romantic.*

But truth is [*checking the clock*] —we're not dead yet.

EL TICHO: Look … We got off on the wrong foot, I agree, but we can work it out.

RÓMULO: I think I broke a few ribs, man.

> *He opens his shirt, revealing a concealable bulletproof vest underneath.* ANGELA *touches the mark the bullet left on it. He winces.*

Ah …! I don't think I'm cut out for the highway patrol.

ANGELA: Take a few deep breaths, / Rómulo.

> *Ignoring* EL TICHO, RÓMULO *takes things out of his jacket pockets—rifle magazine, crisps, sauce sachet—and throws them on the table, then opens his vest.* ANGELA *gently examines where he was hit.*

EL TICHO: Listen, listen, I have a crack offer / for you! The best yet!

RÓMULO: [*to* ANGELA] I'm trying, man.

EL TICHO: I will leave the business for good. I'll disappear. I swear it on my mother's life—

RÓMULO: [*looking at the vest*] This shit actually *works*. Who knew, man?

EL TICHO: Don't you see? I'll give it all away. My house, my family, my money, everything. I am willing to give everything up. Everything I have done, everything I have made. Just don't let them get hold of me.

ANGELA: But, Rómulo, you never wear a vest. How many times—

RÓMULO: No, man, it was lucky Thursday. I always wear it lucky Thursdays.

EL TICHO: Are you *listening* to me, *pendejos*? You don't understand! You think they'll kill me? Don't you see? Don't you get it? [*Bursting into tears*] The house always wins.

They will send me to the North, trussed up tight as a pig on a spit. You don't know these people. They will beat me and torture me and when they've had their fill they'll lock me away in a cellar somewhere to ferment like bootleg *pulque* and I will never see a human face or feel the touch of the sun again. And they will stream the whole thing live for their amusement. I will be their carnival freak, their animal, their beast. Please, I'm begging you, you're my only chance. Don't let them take me North! Kill me, Rómulo! For the love of your girl! Kill me, Angela! For the sake of your father! Pity me, pity me for God's love. *¡Mátenme, por piedad! ¡No dejen que me lleven al Norte! ¡No dejen que me lleve la chingada!*

He howls like a captured beast.

[*Hoarsely, losing force*] You, you're nothing. You're less than nothing. Don't you know who I am? You worthless fuckin' cocksuckers, don't you know who I am?

RÓMULO: [*putting his hand on his shoulder*] Don't matter who you are, old man. Whatever comes flapping through that door, it's coming for *all* of us.

RÓMULO *takes the blanket from his shoulders and drops it on the bed. He and* ANGELA *move around the room securing the accesses and moving the furniture to prepare barricades as they talk.* RÓMULO *reloads the rifle with the magazine. The door is locked but remains accessible.* RÓMULO *stops to recover his breath.*

ANGELA: We need to get you a doctor.

RÓMULO: Nah—I—

ANGELA: You were *shot*, Rómulo. I thought you were dead.

RÓMULO: Me too. Dead looked like my best option for while there. Weird though. All the anger—

ANGELA: Yeah?

RÓMULO: Fizzed away like a leaky tyre. Not pissed 'bout Elisa's future. Just *gutted* not to be there to see it. Man …

He takes out his wallet and looks at the picture of Elisa.

I broke my phone, man.

ANGELA: Here. Try mine.

She passes him her phone. RÓMULO *searches for a signal.*

No luck?

RÓMULO: They'll have blocked it. What's this but?

A video starts to play. We hear shouting voices ... pause ... then the voice of someone: 'Hey, dude, don't you know who I am?'

Holy shit. Where'd you score this, man?

ANGELA: I took a video—

RÓMULO: On your phone. *¡Qué chingón, Lieutenant!* Reckon we could add it to that notebook of yours or somethin'?

ANGELA: Better than that. Put it up on the web. Let's see how the dirt-bag handles some bad publicity.

RÓMULO: Whoa, Boss!

Faint engine sounds in the distance. ANGELA *picks up the clock.*

ANGELA: Hear that? Twenty minutes.

She puts the clock down, but carelessly. For the first time the audience can see it; it shows 11:59.

RÓMULO: Man, and they say time flies when you're having fun.

There is a change in the light. The clock blacks out.

EL TICHO: We're nothing but shadows, ghosts.

ANGELA: Power's cut.

EL TICHO: The darkness is coming.

RÓMULO: [*taking a crisp and squeezing a bit of sauce on it*] One last bite, for luck.

ANGELA holds out her hand; he offers her a carefully selected crisp, squeezing the sachet of sauce on it, like a Eucharist. ANGELA eats it, then starts to cough.

The revving of engines. RÓMULO *crouches by the window.*

ANGELA: Is it the army?

Bullets strike the window. ANGELA *throws herself to the floor.*

RÓMULO: No way, man.

EL TICHO: Thank God, thank God, they're here. I knew they'd come through. [*Shouting viscerally*] My boys love me! Hold your fire, lads, there's only two of them—!

He is interrupted by a hail of bullets. He is hit in the leg, ANGELA *crawls over to assist him.* RÓMULO *jumps to his feet.*

RÓMULO: [*shooting repeatedly through the window*] *Motherfuckers!*
EL TICHO: The fuckin' Young Bloods. But who the fuck—?

{ RÓMULO: Your driver—
{ EL TICHO: Víctor—!

RÓMULO: He said he needed to pick his nose, man. I only untied one
    hand—
EL TICHO: You think it takes two hands to dial a number? No, no, no—
    not *this*, not now. Víctor! *¡Hijo de puta!* I took you in! I made you
    rich!
ANGELA: Rómulo *¡Abajo!*
EL TICHO: Víctor, you gelded prick, you were like a *son* to me!

> *More bullets.* EL TICHO *sits up, quietly moaning.* ANGELA *tears
> a pillowcase.*

RÓMULO: What the fuck, man? Your own people—
EL TICHO: I have no people now.
ANGELA: Brace yourself—

> *She ties the bandage tightly over El Ticho's wound.*

EL TICHO: Congratulations, Lieutenant. The gods have granted your
    wish: I've been taken over. This is the Young Bloods' idea of a sever-
    ance package.

> *Sound of a distant helicopter, very gradually getting closer.*

ANGELA: Don't worry, that's an army helicopter I hear.
EL TICHO: Oh, Angela! What difference will that make? Why should they
    risk their lives when those sadistic bastards out there will do the dirty
    work for them? Do it better, do it cheaper.
RÓMULO: But you're a wanted man.
EL TICHO: No, no, my friend, I am an unwanted man. A nobody.
RÓMULO: Well, join the club.
EL TICHO: Víctor … Víctor … Fuck. *Esperen un momento.*
RÓMULO: This is not another deal, is it? Because I've fuckin' had it up
    to the throat with that shit.
EL TICHO: There's an old tunnel around here. From years back, before
    Víctor was even born, the back-stabbing little cuckoo. I'll take you
    there. If we run into the army, I will be *your* insurance.
ANGELA: You don't fool me, / sir—

EL TICHO: Angela—please. Please listen. Just take my phone, that's all I ask: call Father the moment there is a signal. Warn them. Warn them that Víctor has betrayed me, before it's too late.

ANGELA: No. You brought this on yourself—

EL TICHO: My mother, my grandchildren. They're all I have now. If Víctor leads the Young Bloods right to them—

RÓMULO: Oh, man—

EL TICHO: Do you call that justice, *señora*? Are you ready to die for it—?

ANGELA: If that's what it takes—

EL TICHO: [*pointing to* RÓMULO] And him? You want the girl to lose her father? For what? For this? For them?

RÓMULO: Are you makin' a deal, Boss? It sure sounds like a deal to me.

A standstill, a moment of judgment.

ANGELA: No, it's not a deal, Rómulo. It's a vow. [*To* EL TICHO] You going to cut and run?

EL TICHO: Where to, Angela?

RÓMULO: Yeah, man, how we gonna get past the welcome party?

ANGELA: The fire escape—

RÓMULO: Shit, man, you said we'd break our necks—

ANGELA: Well, I may have exaggerated a little …

She holds out a hand and RÓMULO *gives her the keys. She unlocks* EL TICHO; *he gives her his phone.*

Life is full of surprises, Patricio.

The three of them limp to the door, EL TICHO *in the middle, supported by the other two,* RÓMULO *also in pain. Their silhouettes cast anamorphic shadows on the walls.*

It's raining out there.

EL TICHO: At last a stroke of luck. I could do with a wash.

All hell breaks loose. Searchlights. The rhythmic sound of a helicopter, deafeningly loud. A canister lobs into the room, producing a searing bright light. Smoke and fire fills the room. RÓMULO *seems transfixed until pulled away. In the noise and chaos, they start to exit.*

RÓMULO: What's our story, Boss?

ANGELA: What?

RÓMULO: When they ask us what happened here. What we gonna say?

EL TICHO: We say nothing, nothing at all—

ANGELA: And we say it together.

> *Blackout. Rapid fire gunshots, loud and close. The noise of the helicopter fades into the sound of wings flapping as in the start of Scene One.*
>
> *All three appear, like ghosts or shadows, in three separate spotlights.*

RÓMULO: There's not much left to say. Patricio Jesús Hortensio Prieto Chávez, aka El Ticho, is rotting in some stinking prison cell in the North. As for the Young Bloods, well—business has never been better.

EL TICHO: Lieutenant Angela Bassols Guzmán shared my journey, more or less. She was given a dishonourable discharge after the police found her guilty of failing to follow orders. She moved to the North where she works, undocumented, as a cashier in a supermarket. The Northern snow she loves and hates, its touch bruises and soothes her aching memories.

ANGELA: Rómulo García Hernández planned to flee across the border with his daughter. He never made it. He disappeared a few days after El Ticho was captured. The police found his car riddled with bullets, but no trace of him except a spot on the driver's seat, stained red as red as blood. Elisa waits for him every day, her hope like a sickness she cannot shake—

EL TICHO: The Black Witch never sleeps.

ANGELA: A father is a shadow, a sacrifice. A trust.

RÓMULO: It's a risky business, man, but all business is risky, am I right?

THE END

GLOSSARY

¡Abajo!: Literally, 'down'. This adverb usually replaces the imperative form of the verb *bajar* (*¡baja!*) to convey the order 'lie down'. See also *¡vas p'abajo, cabrón!*

Altiplano: A high plateau. Many important cities across Latin America were founded in high plateaux that had access to sources of water—for example, El Alto (Bolivia); Bogotá and Medellín (Colombia); Mexico City, Guanajuato and Puebla (Mexico); and Juliaca and Puno (Perú).

¡Ay cabrón!: A vulgar interjection that expresses surprise, such as 'oh geez!', or 'oh heck!'. See also *cabrón* and *¡vas p'abajo, cabrón!*

Basta: Enough. See also *¡Ya basta!*

Cabrón: Literally, a buck or billy. The term can be used, depending on the intention of the speaker, either as an insult or as an adjective qualifying something extremely surprising. See also *ay cabrón* and *¡vas p'abajo, cabrón!*

Calaca: In Mexico, colloquial noun used to refer to a human skeleton.

¡Cállate!: Shut up!

Carajo: Damn it!

Centavo: Cent.

Chicas: Girls.

Chinga tu madre: Literally, 'go and rape your mother'. It is an extremely offensive insult that emerged at the time of Conquest, because of the high number of Indian women who were raped by the Spanish conquerors.

Cholo: In its origins, a derogatory term for interracial descendants in the Spanish Empire and its successor states in Latin America. *Cholos* were culturally marginal *mestizos*—persons of mixed European and Indigenous (and sometimes African) descent. Even though *cholo* no longer necessarily refers only to ethnic heritage and not always entails a derogatory sense, it still conveys negative racial and cultural stereotypes when the speaker uses it as a grievous insult. In northern

Mexico, for example, *cholo* designates members of gangs. In some South American countries (e.g. Bolivia or Perú), *cholo* implies servitude and acculturation in people of Amerindian racial ancestry if the speaker uses it with contempt.

Claro: Literally, 'clear'. When used by itself in affirmative form, a short way of expressing 'I get it'.

Corrido: A popular ballad that addresses oppression, the struggle of underprivileged classes, revolution and other relevant social themes. The *narcocorrido* is a subgenre of the *corrido* that describes the lives of the poor, the destitute, and those who seek power through illegal means—mainly, via drug trafficking.

¡Dios mío!: My God!

¿Dónde chingados está mi gente?: Where the fuck is my people?

Esperen un momento: Wait a moment.

Entendido: Literally, 'understood'. In the interrogative form, it is a short way of asking 'Do you understand?' In affirmative form, a short way of stating 'I understood'.

¿Está claro?: Is that clear? See also *claro*.

Indio: General vocative for Amerindians. Even though it is possible to use the term in a neutral form, it historically developed a negative meaning in the Spanish colonial context. The paternalistic structure of the colonial regime regarded *indios* as '*rústicos y miserables*' (i.e. uneducated and indigent, and therefore required of special protection from the Crown). Nowadays, the preferred term to refer to Amerindians is *indígena* (Indigenous). See also *indio ladino*.

Indio ladino: A westernised Amerindian. The word is derived from the old Spanish *ladino*, originally referring to Jews or Muslims who spoke Romance languages in medieval times, and later also developing the separate meaning of 'crafty' or 'astute'. In the Central American colonial context, it was first used to refer to those Amerindians who came to speak only Spanish and later included their *mestizo* descendants, thus developing the racialised meaning of 'untrustworthy'.

¡Hasta luego!: See you later!

¡Hijo de puta!: Son of a bitch!

Huevos: Literally, 'eggs'. This noun is used across Spanish-speaking countries as a vulgar designation for testicles.

Jefe, jefa: Boss.

La bruja negra: The black witch. See also *la mariposa de la muerte*.

La mariposa de la muerte: The butterfly of death. In Mexico, sighting a black moth in one's home represents either a recently deceased loved one visiting the living, or an omen of impending death for someone who is ill. See also *la bruja negra*.

La puta madre; ¡Tu puta madre!: Literally, 'the whore mother' / 'your whore mother'. This expression indicates extreme annoyance or irritation, similar to the one conveyed by the English phrase 'for fuck's sake'.

La Santa Muerte: Short appellation for *Nuestra Señora de la Santa Muerte* (Our Lady of the Holy Death). In Mexico, she is a folk Catholic female deity or saint associated with healing, protection, financial wellbeing, and assurance of a path to the afterlife. Her devotees believe she can protect them against assaults, accidents, gun violence, and all types of violent death. She also embodies a lethal force directed against rivals and enemies. *La Santa Muerte* is usually represented as a skeleton dressed in female clothes or a shroud, and carrying both a scythe (symbolising her power to cut or terminate life) and a globe (symbolising her dominion over humanity and the earth). In other Latin American countries, such as Argentina, Brazil and Paraguay, *San La Muerte* (Saint Death) is represented as a male skeleton. Despite condemnation by Catholic prelates, the worship of *La Santa Muerte* has become increasingly prominent in the last decades.

La tira: In Mexico, pejorative slang to refer to the police. Apocopated form of *la tirana* (the tyrant). It is analogous to the English expression 'the pigs'. It can refer to a single officer when used in singular form (*el tira*).

Lengua: Tongue.

Loco, loca: The term is both a noun and an adjective. As a noun, it refers to a mad or crazy person. When the term is used as an adjective, it can qualify a person who is crazy (*'Luis está completamente loco'*, i.e. 'Luis is completely crazy'), an act that is risky or imprudent ('*una carrera loca*', i.e. 'a crazy race'), or a situation that is tremendous and terrific ('*una fiesta loca*', i.e. 'a crazy party'). In the play, it is used in the first sense—as an insult.

Los Generales: The (army) generals.

Los muertos no hablan: Dead men tell no tales.

Macana: Club, cudgel. In profane language, this noun refers to masculine genitalia.

Macho: This term, which is used both in Spanish and Portuguese languages, derives from the Latin *mascŭlus*, meaning male. *Macho* conveys an Iberian ideal of masculinity that encompasses bravery, courage and strength as well as wisdom and leadership. In the 1960s and 1970s, however, Latin American feminists began using the term to describe male aggression, violence and toxic masculinity. The original positive sense of the term has thus somehow eroded, so it is used today to point out the particularities of Iberian and Latin American brands of patriarchy.

Matador: Bullfighter.

¡Mátenme, por piedad!: Kill me, for pity's sake!

Medallita: A small medallion which generally has a religious icon (e.g. an image of the Virgin or a saint) carved in it.

Mi pequeña torera: My little (female) bullfighter.

¡Mierda!: Shit!

Mirrey: Literally, 'my king'. In Mexico, pejorative slang to refer to an arrogant young white man from an affluent family. It is a contemptuous form of 'my lord'.

Moto: Motorcycle.

Muchacha: Girl.

Mula: A mule or courier who transports illegal drugs across borders.

Nada: Nothing, zilch.

¡No dejen que me lleven al Norte!: Don't let them take me to the North!

¡No dejen que me lleve la chingada!: Literally, 'don't let *la chingada* take me away'. In Mexico, *chingada* is a colloquial or crass noun (depending on the intention of the speaker) that refers to various conditions or situations of, generally, negative connotations. In this case, *chingada* refers to an exceptionally dreadful situation, so we could translate this phrase as 'don't let the fucking hell take me away'. While the feminine form *chingada* communicates a negative state of affairs or emotion, the masculine form *chingón* expresses positive emotions and empowerment. See also *Chinga tu madre* and *¡Qué chingón!*

No mames: Literally, 'don't suck it'. A Mexican vulgar idiom that expresses disbelief, excitement or surprise, both in positive and negative tones. This expression corresponds to English idioms such as 'Holy shit!', 'No way!', 'You're kidding me!', or 'Stop messing with me!'

No importa: It doesn't matter.

No sea igualado: This expression vindicates the speaker's higher social hierarchy, relative to the person addressed, in terms of race, age, rank or class. It can be translated either as 'I am not like you', 'You and I are not the same', or 'Don't you dare to compare yourself with me'.

Paliacate: A brightly coloured handkerchief or bandana that, when used to garnish the neck or cover the head, is associated with the Zapatistas.

Pendejo: Stupid, imbecile. Except for Argentina and Uruguay, where the term is used to refer to children or teenagers, in the rest of Latin American countries *pendejo* is both a derogatory and vulgar word, analogous to English expressions such as 'arsehole' or 'dumbass'.

Pepenadores, buzos, chatarreros: Terms used across Latin America to refer to waste pickers or scavengers who salvage to sell or for personal consumption reusable or recyclable materials thrown away by others (usually in a landfill).

Pimiento: Capsicum. '*Me importa un pimiento*' corresponds to the English idiom 'I do not give a damn'.

¡Ponte buzo!: Watch out, dipstick!

¡Por Dios!: For God's sake!

¡Por favor!: Please! In the context of a discussion, this phrase does not express courtesy, but exasperation.

Prohibido fumar: No smoking.

Puercos: Pigs.

Pulque: An alcoholic beverage made from the fermented sap of the maguey plant. Before the Spanish colonisation of the Americas, *pulque* was used for religious ceremonies in Mesoamerica, but after the Spanish conquest, *pulque* consumption lost its ritual meanings. *Pulque* is still consumed in Mexico, mostly in rural and poor areas. It has acquired a general connotation of being a beverage for the lower classes.

¡Qué chingón!: *Chingón* is a crass noun that conveys extremely positive circumstances or feelings when coupled with the pronoun *que*. This phrase can be translated to English as 'Awesome!', or 'This is great!'

¡Qué te jodan!: Fuck you!

Salsa Adelita: An imaginary Latin American brand of hot sauce, such as *Valentina*, *Melinda*, *Cholula*, *Tamazula* or *Légal*.

Señor: Sir, mister.

Señora: Madame, lady. Generally used as a vocative for mature or married women.

Sicario: Hitman, hired killer.

Taquería: A restaurant that specialises in tacos and other Mexican dishes.

Telenovela: A television serial drama or soap opera.

Te lo ruego: I'm begging you.

Tengo derechos, señor: I have rights, sir.

¿Tú me entiendes, verdad?: You understand me, don't you?

¡Vas p'abajo, cabrón!: You're going down, arsehole!

Viejo pendejo: Stupid old man. See *pendejo*.

¡Ya basta!: That's enough! (expressed with significant emphasis). See also *basta*.

▼ ▼ ▼ ▼ ▼

THE STREET PRESENTS

TWENTY MINUTES WITH THE DEVIL
BY LUIS GÓMEZ ROMERO & DESMOND MANDERSON

CURRENCY PRESS

World Premiere Season at The Street Theatre, Canberra
21–29 August 2021

Supported by

ACT Government

GOVERNMENT ACKNOWLEDGEMENTS
This project is made possible with the support of the ACT government.

THE STREET

THE STREET COMPANY

Artistic Director/CEO	Caroline Stacey
Executive Producer	Dean Ellis
Arts Program Producer	Shelly Higgs
Communications-Publicity	Su Hodge
Technical Manager	James Tighe
Front of House	Pierce Craswell
	Lilia Walsh
Evening	Logan Craswell
	William Malam
Brand and graphic design	DAMS
Photography	Creswick Collective
	Shelly Higgs

STREET BOARD
Mark Craswell (Chair), Susan Blain (Deputy Chair), Susana Fior (Treasurer), Kate Shepherd (Secretary), Penny Calvert, Christina Graves

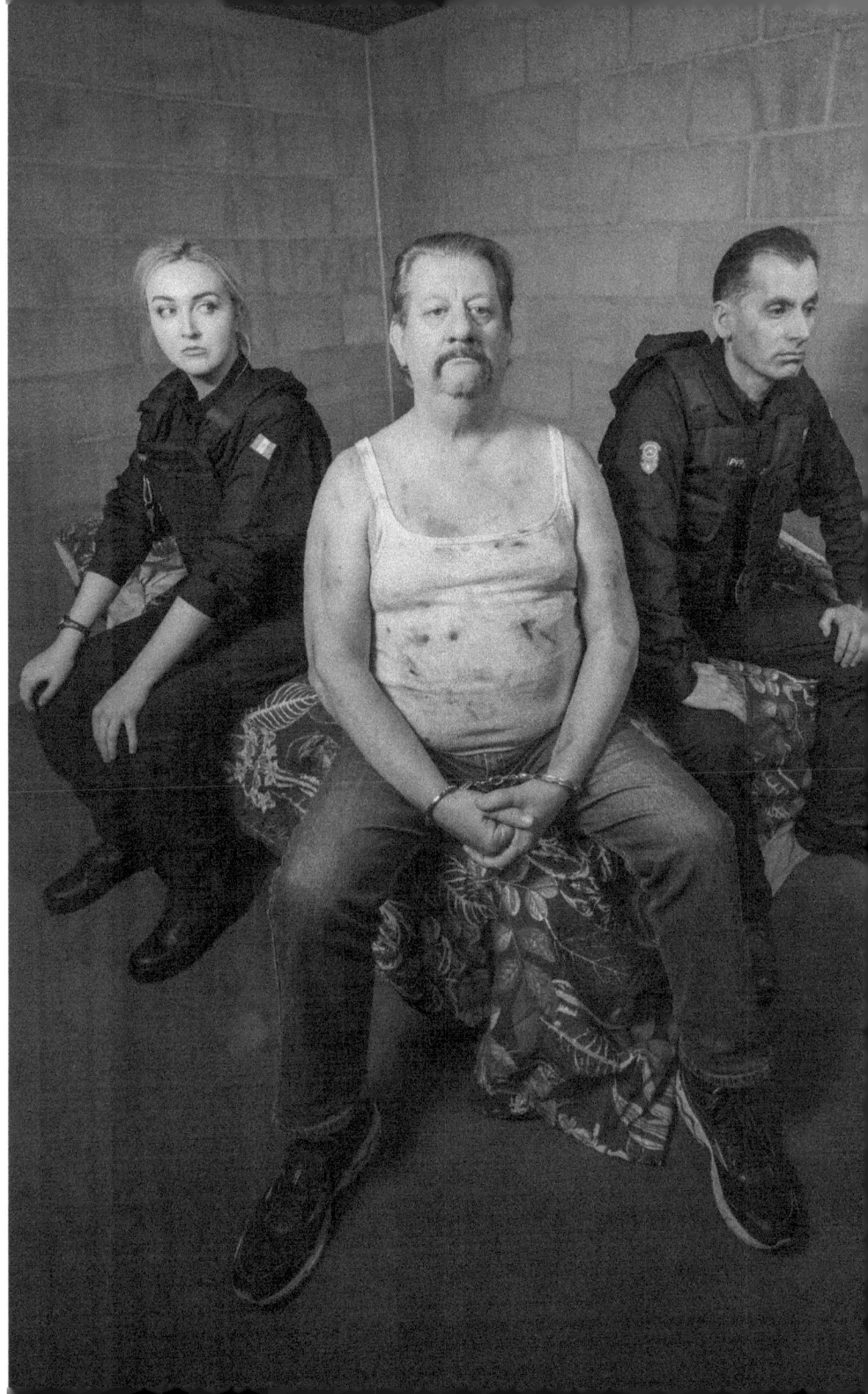

PRODUCTION

Cast

El Ticho	PJ Williams
Angela Bassols Guzmán	Joanna Richards
Rómulo García Hernández	Raoul Craemer

Creative Team

Director	Caroline Stacey
Production Design	Imogen Keen
Sound Design	James Tighe
Lighting Design	Antony Hateley
Movement	Zsuzsi Soboslay

Production Team

Stage Manager	Brittany Myers
Lighting Operator	William Malam
Sound Operator	James Tighe
Set Construction	Tony Theobold
Publicity	Su Hodge
Marketing Artwork	DAMS
Production Photography	Creswick Collective
Social Media	DAMS

Scenes

Scene 1: The Hospitality Business
Scene 2: Outgunned
Scene 3: Temptation
Scene 4: Judging the Devil
Scene 5: The Quetzal
Scene 6: Coming for All of Us

FROM THE WRITERS

The storyteller: This work was born from intellectual commitment and a personal life experience mediated by the myth of the big, bad (Mexican) drug trafficker. We were driven to theatre because, in our academic practice, we have always connected the arts and culture to the description and critique of how law, as a technique of justice, relates to the demands of social life. Growing up in Mexico, I also witnessed first-hand the prehistory of the Mexican drug war and its bewildering development into the unfathomable violence that curses my birth country today. As a Mexican immigrant, I am haunted by the representation of token sadistic "bad hombres" who threaten the world with poisonous drugs. The story we tell challenges these prejudices by situating the drug wars as an episode in a broader and deeper global crisis of justice.

The poet: This work comes out of a life-long passion for the theatre and a life-long belief that the humanities, arts and culture, are indispensable to how we think about law and justice in the modern world. The story we have tried to tell here takes as its starting-point real events in the global war on drugs, and the terrible costs that so-called war is exacting on people and on whole societies around the world. But we also saw it as a modern fairy tale, a parable for the many crises – of politics, of inequality, of power – that confront us: in Australia no less than elsewhere. We have tried to create characters and a language – an idiom – that captures a world in translation; a world that is both like and unlike our own, familiar and yet suddenly strange, like a picture viewed from a surprising angle. Our use of language does not attempt to efface the differences between cultures and societies but to immerse the audience in them.

The poet & the storyteller: Above all, we wanted to tell a story that felt real and surprising, comic and tragic, exciting and memorable. Of course, what we barely appreciated at the time was how much this story would be transfigured by the touch of the many creative talents at The Street, from actors and designers to directors, who have brought our words to life; and how much their imagination and commitment has transformed us too.

Luis Gómez Romero and Desmond Manderson
Canberra July 2021

FROM THE DIRECTOR

Law academics Desmond Manderson and Luis Gómez Romero first approached me four years ago with an utterly compelling idea for a play inspired by the capture of Mexico's most notorious drug lord El Chapo. They spoke to me of Latin America in the context of the global American-driven war on drugs, the crisis of justice in the modern world, the ever-widening gap between law and justice, growing corruption and unfathomable violence, and our individual responsibility when we opt for willful blindness in the face of the disaster.

When I asked 'why theatre? they spoke of the arts as lenses for writing about law and justice in their own academic work but that this idea demanded they write a theatre work. And the idea? The most wanted man in the world is picked up by a couple of highway cops for speeding. Two crummy cops and the most wanted man in the world locked in a hotel room together in the middle of the desert? The army's coming, the cartel's coming. No-one knows who's going to live and who's going to die. What did they say to each other? What did they think about justice? I was hooked.

Over time the play emerged as a black comedy meets thriller meets magical realism. A fairytale where the living dance with the dead. But also a narco narrative that talks directly to race, class, gender, and the 'Atlantic gaze' rejecting mainstream narco tropes of the bad Mexican cop, the good Mexican cop, and the sadistic, whimsical narco. However the world created is not Mexico. It is everywhere and nowhere. There is The North and The South and The Border. The Centre and the Periphery. Created is a world like and unlike our own, familiar and strange, peppered with Spanish and English, filled with ghosts and hauntings, producers and consumers, symbols and myths, fragility and violence, madness, family and fathers. The locked motel room is the locked room of the modern world and the clock is ticking for all of us. *Twenty Minutes with the Devil* moves through absurdity, rage, despair, hope, fear, love and betrayal. It asks what you believe in when you think you are about to die. Des and Luis have written a play that is extraordinary, rich and complex. It goes to the heart of deeply personal moral decisions in communities crippled by the nonchalant arrogance of imperial powers. And it reveals the solidarity that can emerge from uncertainty.

It has been an extraordinary journey for our community of artists and we have learned much about ourselves and justice in the process.

Caroline Stacey
Canberra 2021

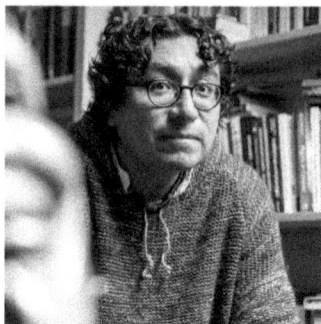

LUIS GÓMEZ ROMERO
Playwright

Luis Gómez Romero was born and raised in Mexico where, under the canopy of tangerine and lemon sunsets, he learnt to love justice and beautifully crafted stories. In Mexico, he passionately worked for structuring peaceful alternatives to reduce the harm caused by violent drug prohibitionism. He turned to academic life believing it was his personal route to a serene and joyful Mexican Ithaca. Academia, however, eventually became his path to Australia, where he arrived in 2013. Luis is currently a senior lecturer at the School of Law at the University of Wollongong. In Australia, his academic work addresses the intersections between law, justice and culture, particularly in Latin American contexts. Luis is a frequent media commentator on Latin American law and politics. He has written with Desmond Manderson his first play, in collaboration with The Street Theatre, on a story that is both political and deeply personal – because the contemporary history of the violence unleashed by the Mexican drug war is also the story of Luis' Antipodean exile.

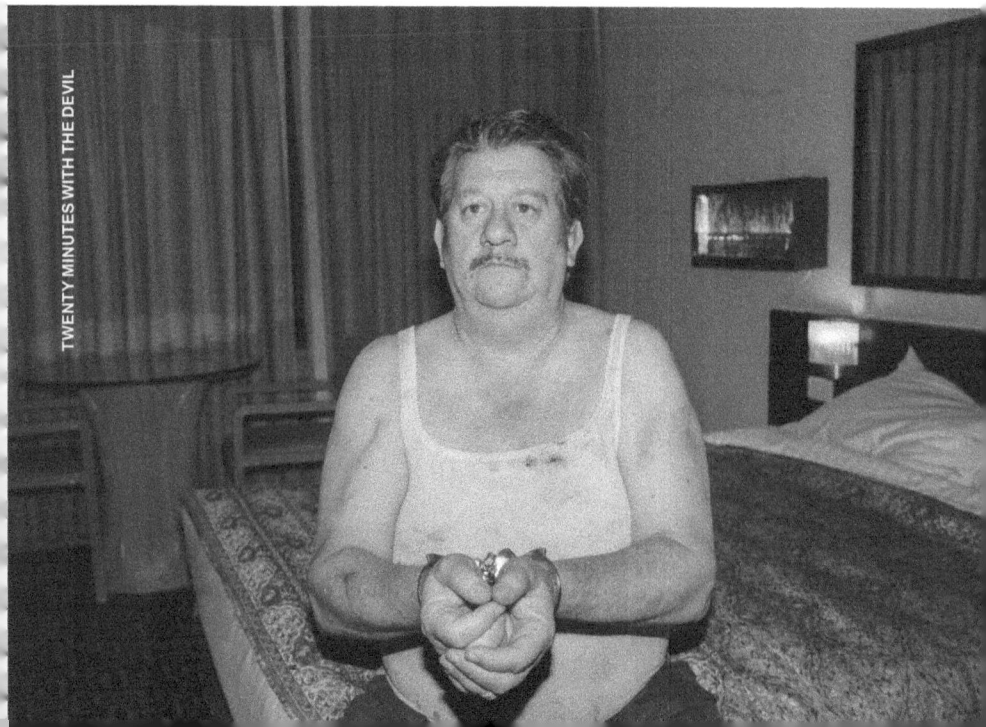

DESMOND MANDERSON
Playwright

In his salad days, Desmond Manderson was a playwright and a musician, before turning to academic life. His books are known around the world for their pioneering approach to exploring questions of law and justice through music, literature, history, philosophy, and art. In Australia he is a frequent commentator in newspapers and on the radio, with diverse interests ranging from social justice, drug policy and ethics, to food and contemporary art. As a Professor jointly appointed in the ANU College of Law and the College of Arts & Social Sciences, and as Director of the Centre for Law, Arts and Humanities, he has developed many innovative cross-campus teaching and research initiatives. His commitment to connect ideas, art, and culture has led to work with the National Library, the National Gallery, Heide, and now The Street Theatre—returning, at long last, to his first love.

CAROLINE STACEY
Director

Caroline Stacey is the Artistic Director/CEO of award-winning creative powerhouse, The Street – Canberra's leading creative producer of contemporary theatre and live performance and the creative hub for professional and independent artists. A multi-award winning director in 2012 Caroline received the Canberra Artist of the Year Award for her outstanding contribution to theatre and the performing arts. Caroline has an extensive career as a festival director leading Castlemaine State Festival for seven years and as a stage director of theatre and opera working for companies as diverse as West Australian Opera, Adelaide Symphony Orchestra, Melbourne International Arts Festival, Sydney Opera House, Queensland Music Festival, Victorian Opera, Canterbury Opera, Melbourne Opera, Saltpillar Theatre, and Downstage Theatre (NZ). Works directed for The Street include: *Breaking The Castle*; *Flight Memory*; *A Doll's House, Part 2*; *Venus in Fur*; *Diary of a Madman*; *The Weight of Light*; *Boys Will Be Boys*; *Cold Light*; *Constellations*; *The Chain Bridge*; *The Faithful Servant*; *MP*; *To Silence*; *The Give and Take*; *Where I End & You Begin*; *Jacques Brel is Alive and Well and Living in Paris*; *Dido and Aeneas*; *Capital, Medea*; *The Jade Harp*; *Albert Herring*; *The Six Memos*; and *From A Black Sky*.

PJ WILLIAMS
Actor / *El Ticho*

PJ Williams is an actor and director. He has been involved with The Street Theatre's Hive Writing Program and First Seen as a workshop director, dramaturge and actor. PJ was a co-founder of Impro Theatre ACT. Acting credits include: *A Doll's House, Part 2*; *The Diary of a Madman*, *The Faithful Servant*; *The Chain Bridge*; *Late Night Catechism*; *Violine*; *Under One Roof*; *Six Pack*; *Breathing Corpses*; *The Give and Take*; *Without Prejudice*. TV credits include appearances in: *Home & Away*; *All Saints*; *Always Greener*; and *Tricky Business* plus numerous commercials. Directing credits for The Street include: *Grimm & The Blue Crown Owl* (opera); *Laurie & Shirley* (a play in verse); *Lies, Love & Hitler*; and *War of The Worlds* as well as a number of workshop developments. In 2008 he received the MEAA Actors Equity award for Professional Practice and in 2016 and 2018 Canberra Critics Circle Award for his performances in *Faithful Servant* and *Diary of a Madman*. PJ has been a proud member of Actors Equity (MEAA) since 1989. PJ has worked with ABC Canberra as a freelance media practitioner since 2002. He is a current board member of the National Folk Festival and a former board member of The Street.

JOANNA RICHARDS
Actor / *Angela*

Joanna Richards trained at American Repertory Theatre at Harvard with Moscow Art Theatre Conservatory, where she played Natasha in *Three Sisters* and Yelena in *Uncle Vanya*. Stage credits in Canberra include; Vanda in *Venus in Fur*; Harrison in *Boys Will Be Boys*; Atajara in *Widowbird* (The Street Theatre); Ellen in *Belfast Girls* (Echo Theatre); Hero in *Much Ado About Nothing* (Lakespeare); and various music theatre works at QCC including *Blood Brothers* and *Fame*, both directed by Stephen Pike. Screen credits include Judy in *Rake* (Blow by Blow) and Sarah in *Whirld* (2Kats). Joanna is a keen screenwriter and playwright. She was fortunate to be selected for The Street Theatre's Early Phase, WIFT's Mentor Her program, and a mentorship with Chips & Gravy Production company. Outside of the theatre, Joanna is the first PhD Candidate in Virginia Haussegger's 50/50 by 2030 foundation. She frequently provides comment and opinion for various print, radio and television programs on issues relating to women's representation and rights.

TWENTY MINUTES WITH THE DEVIL

RAOUL CRAEMER
Actor / *Rómulo*

Raoul Craemer grew up in Germany and India and trained as an actor on a UK Dance and Drama Award at ArtsEd London (MA in Acting, 2003). He has over 25 credits in theatre and film and has written three plays: his solo show *Pigman's Lament* (2016); *Destination Home* (2011); and *Vidooshaka – The Indian Clown* (2004). For his solo performance as the medieval Indian weaver-poet *Kabir* (2012), his professional peers awarded him a Green Room Award as Professional Performer of the Year. On film, Raoul most recently played Michael Curtiz, the Hollywood director who discovered Errol Flynn in the biopic *In Like Flynn* which ran in cinemas worldwide in 2018 (dir. Russell Mulcahy). Raoul has combined his experience as an actor and playwright with his prior training in economics (MPhil, Oxford University) to become one of a handful of arts economists in Australia. He is Senior Director of the Policy Design and Evaluation team in the ACT Government's Chief Minister, Treasury and Economic Development Directorate, where he leads capacity building in evaluation for the ACT Public Service. He has previously also been the Treasurer for the ACT Writers Centre, and a Board Member for the ACT's Cultural Facilities Corporation.

IMOGEN KEEN
Costume and Set

Imogen Keen is an award-winning set and costume designer for professional theatre production. She has enjoyed a long collaboration with The Street Theatre, including design for: *Milk*; *Breaking The Castle*; *Flight Memory*; *Fragments*; *Metamorphosis*; *A Doll's House, Part 2*; *Venus in Fur*; *Diary of a Madman*; *The Weight of Light*; *Boys Will Be Boys*; *Under Sedation: Canberra verse Remixed*; *Constellations*; *Cold Light*; *The Faithful Servant*; *The Chain Bridge*; *MP*; *Where I End & You Begin*; *The Give & Take*; *To Silence*; *Jacques Brel is Alive and Well and Living in Paris*; *Lawrie and Shirley*; *Albert Herring*; *Dido and Aeneas*. Imogen has received Canberra Critics Circle Awards for Theatre Design (2009; 2011) and an MEAA Peer Acknowledgement Award (2011). She has worked on a wide variety of theatre, film, music and cross-disciplinary productions for: Aspen Island Theatre Company; This Band Will Self Destruct; COUP Canberra; Handel In The Theatre; Barking Spider Visual Theatre; Polyglot Theatre; Canberra Youth Theatre; Little Dove Theatre and Urban Theatre Projects. Imogen graduated from the ANU School of Art in 1993.

ANTONY HATELEY
Lighting

Antony Hateley is a Lighting Designer until recently based in London, working in the dance and theatre industry, his work having featured both nationally and internationally. Now based in the ACT he trained in fine art at University of Central England specialising in film and sculpture. A selection of the artists and organisations Antony has previously worked for includes Rambert, Ivan Putrov, Sadler's Wells Theatre, Dance Art Foundation, London College of Fashion, Viviana Durante Company, Botis Seva, Martin Creed, Van Huynh Company, Breakin' Convention, East London Dance, Akademi, Boy Blue Entertainment, Company Decalage and Avant Garde Dance. Through organisations in the UK such as Sadler's Wells Theatre, East London Dance and Breakin' Convention Antony has been involved in many artistic development programs providing nurture and support for new and emerging artists. In addition to lighting design Antony provides production management for both national and international touring productions.

JAMES TIGHE
Sound

James Tighe is a sound designer, production manager, and audio engineer from rural New South Wales, now based in Canberra, and has been working professionally in the live performance industry since graduating from the Australian National University's School of Music in 2014. James has been involved in a range of theatrical productions and musical theatre performances including: sound designer for *Fragments* (The Street 2019); *Exclusion* (The Street 2018); *Miss Saigon* (ANU IHP 2015); and *Ali MacGregor's Alchemy* (Hayes Theatre Co 2015); audio systems designer for *In the Hanging Garden NYE Party* (MONA 2020); audio engineer for MONA FOMA (2020), Amy Shark (NRL 2020), and Tim Freedman (2019); and Head Audio Technician (Canberra Theatre Centre). James currently is Technical Manager at The Street Theatre, and has worked as production manager for The Merchants of Bollywood Kuwait Tour (ATA Allstar 2019), and assistant production manager for The Bar at Buena Vista (ATA Allstar 2018).

WILLIAM MALAM
Lighting Operator

William Mallam started doing tech in the amateur theatre scene back in 2013. He initially got into theatre as an actor but quickly developed an interest in the technical side of things. His interest in theatre tech, specifically lighting, led him to do tech with Child Players ACT, Canberra Youth Theatre, Nova Multimedia, and a multitude of smaller companies before eventually settling in at the Street Theatre in 2018 and working on shows including: *Milk*; *Tourmaline*; *Flight Memory*; *Breaking The Castle*; and *St Nicholas*. When he's not working at the Street William spends his time either fixing his ever broken 1983 Toyota Celica, tinkering with old electronics such as cassette decks, laserdisc players and gameboys, or going to CIT for a Cert IV in Programming.

BRITTANY MYERS
Stage Manager

Brittany Myers graduated with a Bachelor of Communications (Theatre/Media) from Charles Sturt University. She predominantly is a stage manager, but also has credits as an actor, devisor and costumer. With roots in children's theatre, beginning at Sydney's Marian Street Theatre for Young People in 2012, Brittany has a passion for brining engaging shows to all kinds of audiences. Her recent stage management credits include: *Milk* (The Street Theatre 2021); *The Shape of Things* (Flightpath Theatre 2021); *Good Mourning* (Old 505 Theatre, 2020); *Wunderage* (Circus Oz, 2019); *A Midsummer Night's Dream* (Charles Sturt University, 2019); *Bound* (Charles Sturt University, 2018). She relocated to Canberra in 2021, and this is her second show with The Street Theatre.

ZSUZSI SOBOSLAY
Movement

Zsuzsi Soboslay is an award-winning writer, director and movement artist engaged in theatre, education and community cultural development for over 25 years. She has worked in London and Australia with artists of all disciplines, youth, very young children, and adults of all abilities. Works include *The Chain Bridge* (actor); movement consultant (*Cold Light*), director *The Story of The Oars* [online] all for The Street, 2015-20; and as performer-devisor, *Anthems and Angels* (Street Theatre) and *The Compassion Plays* (AGAC), 2014-16.

Zsuzsi has created performance animations for galleries in Canberra and Sydney, teaches stagecraft and embodiment processes to musicians [Sydney Conservatorium; Synergy Percussion] and created the intergenerational *Moon Stories* [ACT Heritage Award 2018] and *The Culture Hub* (2019) with local South Sudanese in 2019. This year, she initiated the ReStorying Project, an arts-centred restorative process open to all artists affected by Covid-19 in partnership with The Street.

www.bodyecology.com.au #creativerestore.

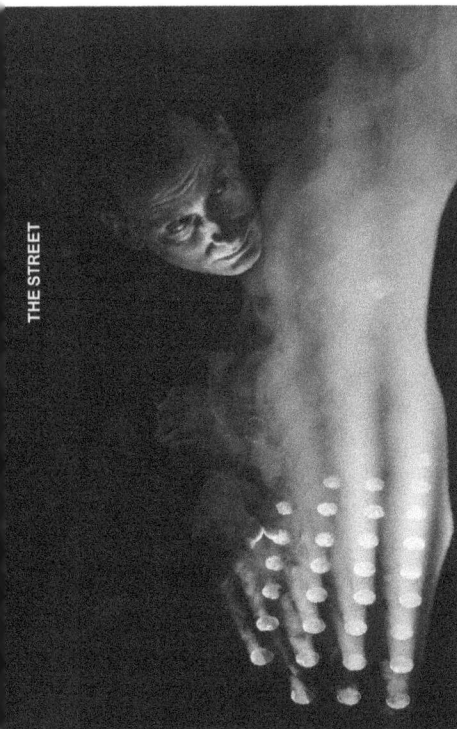

ABOUT THE STREET

The Street Theatre is Canberra's award-winning home of live storytelling and performance in the ACT. An essential part of Canberra's cultural and imaginative life The Street is a major investor in new theatre and music work in Canberra over the last decade. Just as Canberra is considered a petri-dish for new policies, ideas and cultural products within the broader national landscape, The Street serves a vital role as a key creative generator of new work and regenerator of place and community within the nation's political heart.

Our creative hub, situated between the city and ANU, is a meeting place for people across society providing a space to experience diverse perspectives. As Canberra's leading creative producer we're inspired by our geography, history and people, we champion creative process alongside finished work; rich dialogue with our community, and in our city of ideas, inquisitive artists. We commission, develop, produce and present live performance work that talks to the world we live in now and employ some of the finest and much-loved creative talent in the region as well as from Canberra's creative diaspora.

A creative powerhouse The Street was the recipient of a 2020 Sidney Myer Performing Arts Award for outstanding achievement. The Street is considered an essential Arts Organisation supported by the ACT Government and considered an essential contributor to the well-being of residents in the ACT and artistic vibrancy in the region.

WWW.THESTREET.ORG.AU

FIND US

Search
#thestreetcbr

Twitter
@thestreetcbr

Facebook
/thestreettheatre

6247 1223
thestreet.org.au
15 Childers St
Canberra City

ACKNOWLEDGEMENTS

The Street thanks the following people for their contribution to the development of *Twenty Minutes With The Devil*: actors Christopher Carroll, Raoul Craemer, Catherine Crowley, Frank Madrid, Joanna Richards, Karina Salgado, and PJ Williams; dramaturg Peter Matheson and members of The Hive.

A special thank you to Dr Barrie Stacey for his dramaturgical work, insights, and advice

Sam Tonkins for handcuff making.

A huge thanks to gunsmith Bruce Brown and the Shooters Wholesale Warehouse for working as a consultant on this project. For making and providing the guns and accessories used in the production, for training the actors in gun-handling, and for his insights into the respect and care use of these weapons demand.

The writers thank the ANU and the Legal Intersections Research Centre at University of Wollongong, for assistance, both financial and otherwise, they have provided to a most unusual project. Thanks to Caroline Stacey: over our remarkable journey she has been with us and guided us every step of the way. Thanks to the actors who enriched, by their generosity and creativity, the lives of our characters. To Jackie and Macarena, we could not have done it without you. To our daughters, Mariana and Laurence, from their fathers: we love you now
and forever.

Production Sponsor

THE STREET ♡ SUPPORTERS

With thanks for the support of the ANU and University of Wollongong.

Australian National University

Legal Intersections Research Centre

CURRENCY PRESS

THE STREET

THE STREET DONORS

STREET-LIFE ($5,000 +)
Michael Adena, Joanne Daly

STREET-PARTY ($1,000 - $5,000)
Mark Craswell, David & Margaret Williams, Cathy Winters, Peter Wise, Michael Sassella, Shannon Van Den Berg, Anonymous

STREET-WORKS ($500 – $1,000)
Jamie Hladky, Bridget Sack, Caroline Stacey, Colin Neave, Anonymous

STREET-STYLE ($250 - $500)
Shirley Wells, Ilona Di Bella, Bren Wetherstone, Anonymous

STREET-WISE (UP TO $250)

Joan Adler, Catherine Bannister Kate Bosser, Cynthia Bryson, Andrea Close, Catherine Crowley, Margaret Daly, Erin Daly, Shirani Del Mel, Mandy Doherty, Miles Farwell, Nigel Featherstone, Kris Frazer, Stephen Frost, Carey Gaul, Ian Gordon, Fiona Gunn, Beverly Hart, Su Hodge, Graeme Hoy, Margaret Huddy, Eric Huttner, Subhash Jaireth, Gary James, Chris Johnstone, Mahbouhbeh Kamalpou, Carol Kee, Karen Malam, Neil McAlister, Christine Mercer, Rosamund Murn, Angalee Nagodavinthane, Glenda Naughton, Matthew Noble, Ruth Pieloor, Kristin Ritchie, Jennifer Rivers, Margaret Rivers, Fran Romano, Lis Shelly, Catherine Tait, Judy Tier, Anne Treleaven, Nicky Tyndale-Biscoe, Colleen Van Den Berg-Prescott, Femke Withag, Anonymous

To find out more about supporting The Street Theatre please call 02 6247 1519 or visit www.thestreet.org.au/support-us

www.ingramcontent.com/pod-product-compliance
Lightning Source LLC
Chambersburg PA
CBHW050020090426
42734CB00021B/3356